Yorkshire Battles

55p.

11s.

Other "popular" studies of the northern past:

FOLK LORE OF THE LAKE COUNTIES
GHOSTS OF THE LAKE COUNTIES
HAUNTED YORKSHIRE
LEGENDS OF THE LAKE COUNTIES
YORKSHIRE LEGENDS

Printed and bound in Great Britain by
FRETWELL & BRIAN LTD.
Silsden, Nr. Keighley, Yorkshire.

Yorkshire Battles

by

William Hebden

with photographs by Patricia Hebden Inch

DALESMAN PUBLISHING COMPANY, LTD.
Clapham (via Lancaster)
Yorkshire.
1971

This is a popular study of battles fought in Yorkshire from Roman times until the Civil Wars. It is written not so much for the academic historian but rather for schoolchildren, students and adults who are inspired by these stirring epochs of English history. The author is well-known as a lecturer and genealogist, and is a former member of the Council of Yorkshire Archaeological Society.

A recent warmonger has referred to "blood, toil, tears and sweat," recognising that bloodshed is an inevitable result of war. We therefore warn but make no apology for the fact that this book contains references to such features as blood-drenched battlefields, mass executions and the displaying of heads on city walls. To omit details of this kind would be to give an unbalanced picture of an age when savage brutality was part of everyday life.

The author wishes to thank Patricia Hebden Inch for taking the photographs and for assisting in research, and also the numerous reference libraries and record depositories which provided access to documentary material. Reconstructions of battle scenes are by A. Whimperley, maps by Janet Ellerington and the title page decoration by E. Jeffrey.

The front cover depicts Towton Monument and Bloody Meadow, scene of the Battle of Towton in 1461. The Battle of Marston Moor, fought to the west of York, has been omitted from the map on the back cover.

Contents

GATE TO THE MOOR.

Echo for ever on this English field.
For ever echo here you souls of men who scorned to yield.
Wave high the grasses, stirring the flowers fair,
A nation's sons beneath an azure shield,
Lie silent, gathered there.

Ever through history shall your tale unfold,
Ever through history, your fame be told,
Lives there in England still your spirit strong,
In England still, your radiant battle song.
Or lives a leader who, for England's sake,
Would rise once more and such a judgement make.

The author on a battlefield, 1964.

1: *Introduction*

NO county in England has perhaps been so steeped in battles as Yorkshire. Nor is the reason far to seek, for it may well be claimed that from earliest times, whoever held the north held England. From end to end of Britain's most famous highway, the Great North Road, have come down many stories of ancient battles, but among these none has been so sanguinary or final as those fought north of Yorkshire's southern borders. Many of the earliest Yorkshire battles have not been fully recorded, for statistics have been few. Lost in a maze of antiquity, many such battles today emerge merely as lines in old ballads, legends or words in our Yorkshire language—descriptions such as Bloody Field, Scarlet Heights, Dane's Lane, Grim's Dyke, Giant's Dyke, Battle Flats or Trooper Lane. Such names as these, particularly where descended from Celtic, Saxon or Danish times, together with strange marks upon the land, whisper today of stranger happenings.

At Stanwick north of Richmond lie Celtic or early British military earthworks covering some 800 acres and at one time capable of housing 100,000 persons. In the well-known Grasswoods above Grassington, similar marks bear witness to a stronghold of the ancient British tribe of Brigantes, whose Queen, Cartesmandhua, betrayed to the Romans the Celtic hero, Caractacus. On the moors above Wensleydale are deeply trenched earthworks, about which few may speak with complete authority, while the moors along the coast from Whitby to Flamborough afford many examples of ancient methods of attack or defence as well as numerous battlefields. At Gristhorpe, near Scarborough, there was unearthed in 1834 —typical of many such discoveries up and down Yorkshire—a

7

wooden coffin, hacked from a tree trunk and housing the skeleton of a warrior complete with weapons of some bygone age. Stretching away from Scarborough above Lockton, Levisham and Pickering are many similar relics, and at Saltersgate there exists an old-time entrenchment known as "Double Dykes," a mile in length and still in excellent preservation. At Cawthorne, Blakey and Ebberston there are many traditions of mighty struggles during ancient times. Thus, all the way across Yorkshire towards the Lancashire border, one can discover traces of roads or fortifications reminiscent of northern battles of long ago.

Yorkshire battlefields do not confine themselves only to the Celtic, Roman Anglo-Saxon or Danish periods. There still remain—virtually unaltered from descriptions given at the time of the battles themselves—several peaceful looking yet strangely haunted places such as Moor or Bloody Lane, running across Marston Moor since 1644. Another example is Cocksford near Towton, which is still approached by a winding pathway below a hillside that witnessed the deaths of thousands of fugitives from the Battle of Towton in 1461.

Fortunately for the student who may find himself unable to visit Yorkshire's more distant battlefields, almost every known earthwork or entrenchment may be readily traced among scores of maps deposited in reference libraries. While engaged in the study of maps, it may be well to remember that in many cases the older the map the better, since the subject, particularly if adjacent to present day suburbs, is not so likely to have become "fogged" as may be the case with more modern maps incorporating housing estates, arterial highways or ribbon building.

One of the earliest recorded battles ever to have been fought in Yorkshire was that of Heathfield or Hatfield, near Doncaster, in 633 between Penda, heathen King of Mercia, and Edwin, first Christian King of Northumbria. Even this comparatively well remembered battle is today marked only by such names as "Slay Pits" and Stainforth, the "stoneford," by which the armies of King Edwin are reputed to have crossed the river Don. One factor, however, may be gleaned from this ancient battle and its situation among swamps and flats. It may well have occurred to the commanders concerned that while fighting battles on mountain tops may hitherto have been well enough, the use of torrential rivers might be still better. Even today Yorkshire rivers are virtually unapproachable in times of spate, but fifteen hundred years ago marching armies, encumbered by heavy armour or weapons, must have found

Micklegate Bar forms an imposing western entrance to the ancient walled city of York. In medieval times the heads of many rebels, including the Duke of York and Robert Aske, were spiked on its ramparts.

them absolutely impassable. Many an old-time military commander viewing the Aire, Wharfe, Nidd, Ure or Swale, to say nothing of the smaller intersecting streams, may well have turned away in baffled anger.

It was not until some 22 years following the Battle of Hatfield, during which religious hatreds had remained unrestrained, that there was fought a dreadful sequel in the Battle of Winwoed. Situated in the heart of the Kingdom of Elmet—which in those days stretched from Sherburn westwards towards the head waters of Aire, Wharfe and Nidd—Winwoed is clearly traceable. Here in 655 came Penda, victor of Hatfield, to meet in battle King Oswy, grandson of Edwin who had been killed at Hatfield. Penda, leading a great army of Welsh and Mercian warriors, thousands of whom were slain upon the field or drowned in their eventual flight across the swollen river Aire, was killed in company with many of his most famous captains near Barwick. Even in present day times one can re-capture something of this ancient battlefield in an area through which the small Cock Beck—the "cocru" stream of the ancient Britons—still makes its secretive way below ancient earthworks and the modern housing estates of Stanks and Scholes. It flows towards Aberford and Towton, and has twice during eight hundred years run red with blood.

Following the slaying of the King Penda and the merging of the Celtic and Roman Christian churches in 642, there came into being in what is today called Yorkshire, a love of arts, and the writings of such men as the Venerable Bede. Such was the position when, between 790 and 867, waves of invading Danes put thousands of northern Saxons to fire and sword. With the rise of King Alfred the Great, most of the country was swept comparatively clear of Danes, but it remained for King Edward the Elder, son of Alfred, to defeat the northern Danes and afterwards for King Athelstane to smash both Dane and invading Scot at the celebrated Battle of Brunanberg. After this fateful battle the north began to feel a nation—despite its by this time heavily intermingled population of Dane and Saxon.

Unfortunately the accession to the English throne of a foolish Saxon king named Ethelred the Unready—or "without wit"—coincided with invasions by the rapacious Northmen of Ireland and then of Scandinavia, who descended like locusts upon the country. Then came the rule of Canute, a Danish king and the country remained for a time at peace. But when he and his two capable sons died, the Witenagemot or Government of the country had no alternative but to offer the throne to Edward the Confessor, son of the foolish Ethelred who had fled the country on the coming of the Danes. Under this incapable and senile old man, and despite the initiative of his successor, King Harold, there came an end to Saxon England. It was exactly 129 years after the liberating Battle of Brunanberg that the chieftains of Northumbria—and Yorkshire—received news of the expected invasion of England's southern coasts by William the Norman. They learned also of the arrival in the river Humber of thousands of invading Norwegians led by the Scandinavian king, Harald Hardrada, and accompanied by Tostig, rebel Earl of Northumbria. This army of 60,000 lost little time in conquering the city of York. Meanwhile King Harold of England hurried northwards and won such a victory over the Norwegians at Stamford Bridge that they were glad to sail away. It was immediately following this victory that Harold himself, returning southwards to meet the Normans, was slain in the general defeat of Saxon England by William the Conqueror at Hastings in 1066.

Most people know something of the Norman Conquest of England. Away in the south the Saxons were swiftly subdued and submitted to the Conqueror. In the north a different spirit prevailed where Saxon nobles made a strong resistance and William so harried the country that towns stood burned and broken for half a century. For many years following this fearful vengeance, a troubled peace lay over Yorkshire to be broken at last by the Battle of the Standard against the Scottish nation in 1138. A period of almost 200 years was then to elapse before 1320 and the "White Battle of Myton," to be followed in 1322 by the Battle of Boroughbridge, a few months later by the Battle of Byland Abbey and then in 1408 by the Battle of Bramham Moor.

From the time of the Norman Conquest there began to come into being England's famous military castles. To wander across Yorkshire today is to savour these castles to the full. First of such strongholds entering the county from the south is Tickhill, which is still partially moated and one of the five castles licensed for royal tournaments by King Richard I. Many times during English history Tickhill has been the centre of war; it was besieged during the rebellion of Thomas of Lancaster in 1322 and also held by royalists during the Civil Wars. A few miles north of Tickhill, near Rotherham, stands all that is left of the once mighty keep of Conisbrough, a castle which was given by William the Conqueror to the celebrated Norman, William of Warrene. The site is reputed to have been the place of execution and burial of the Saxon

leader, Hengist, in the year 489. North of Conisbrough is Pomfret, poised above the town of Pontefract; a castle which caused Shakespeare to write:

Oh Pomfret, Pomfret, thou bloody prison
Fateful and ominous to noble peers,
Within the guilty closure of thy walls,
Richard the Second here was hacked to death,
Whilst for more slander to thy dismal seat,
We give thee up our guiltless blood to drink.

These words are attributed to Earl Rivers who, with Lord Grey and Sir Thomas Vaughen, was executed at Pomfret in the days of King Richard III. Leaving Pontefract, a very few miles brings one to at least a remnant of the once tremendous castle of Sandal, near Wakefield, from which Richard, Duke of York rode forth during the Wars of the Roses to his death. It is not, however, until several miles further north that it is possible to read the true story of Yorkshire's embattled castles as military seats of war. The squat bulk of Skipton with its still decipherable motto "Desormais"—meaning "Henceforth"—had sister fortresses at Spofforth, Knaresborough, Wressle, Cawood and Londesborough. Midway between all these lies York, with its ancient walls, the tall and graceful Micklegate, Walmgate, Monk and Bootham Bars, a Roman watch tower beside St. Mary's Abbey, and the heights of Clifford's Tower.

Lying a few miles further north, zig-zagging from the hills of Wensleydale towards the coast, run the once mighty strongholds of Bolton, Middleham, Snape, Hornby, Crayke, Sheriff Hutton, Malton, Gilling, Kirkbymoorside, Pickering, Mulgrave and Scarborough. Among these lie lesser strongholds such as Upsall, Kilton and Danby, still-inhabited castles such as Ripley and Hazlewood, and once fortified manor houses such as Markenfield near Ripon. Northwards, although not so far as the once great border castles of Ravensworth, Bowes or Barnard, is the glorious pile of Richmond, castle of Alan the Red.

None of these castles is without its particular story. At Middleham, Warwick the Kingmaker, whose principal home

Opposite: **Implement of ancient warfare. A halberd used in defence against the charging cavalry at the Battle of Marston Moor. (Photo by courtesy of the Castle Museum, York).**

Middleham Castle in Wensleydale is one of the many fortresses whose story is intermingled with that of Yorkshire's battles. Here lived Warwick the Kingmaker and Richard III.

was at Sheriff Hutton, kept a private army of 20,000 men, and here also lived King Richard III "who loved the savage north." In Bolton, prior to the great Catholic insurrection against Queen Elizabeth in 1569, was imprisoned Mary Queen of Scots. At Wressle, Topcliffe and Spofforth lay the great warring family of Percy, Earls of Northumberland; at Skipton that sanguinary House of Clifford which, rampaging through history, spilled its blood upon every battlefield in England and on many a scaffold too.

It was under the rule of such baronial families that there came into Yorkshire during the fifteenth century the so-called Roses' Wars, fought between the rival Houses of York and Lancaster for possession of the English throne. The two most salient of the Roses' battles were firstly the Yorkshire battle of Wakefield and then of Towton Field. Following these gory engagements a hundred years were to elapse before in 1536 came the "Pilgrimage of Grace" under Robert Aske of Aughton, and then in 1569 that Rebellion of the Northern Earls which left its adherents, mostly simple farmers, hanging from gallows trees all the way from Ripon to Darlington. Not for another century did war return to Yorkshire, this time

14

when King Charles I—convinced of the Divine Rights of Kings—made war against his people. It was during these tragic Civil Wars that Yorkshire saw the last of her many battles, firstly in the siege of Bradford, including the Battle of Adwalton Moor between Leeds and Halifax, and secondly among the streets of Leeds around Briggate, Call Lane and Leeds Bridge. Later came the battles of Wakefield, Seacroft, Wetherby, Sherburn, Selby and Tadcaster. Finally and following the siege of Royalist York, was that heart-rending Battle of Marston Moor which, in ending a King's cause in the north, brought ruin to hundreds of Yorkshire homes.

In considering the many Yorkshire families which from time to time have been engaged in war, one is bound to include many quite ordinary surnames. Whenever a fighting baron, knight or squire rode out to war, there marched along with him in feudal obligation the tenants of some village or estate. In seeking the names of Yorkshire's "battle" families, the searcher has various sources including Poll Tax Returns which give the names of the tenants of many estates—muster rolls of ancient battles, lists of confiscations, executions, memoirs of such generals as Sir Thomas Fairfax, parish registers and the like.

When looking at these battles and the people who fought in them, one should not overlook parish churches. Among the most impressive of military tombs to be discovered in such churches are those of the Cliffords at Skipton-in-Craven. At Little Driffield hangs a tablet commemorating Alfried, son of Oswy, King of Northumbria, who died in battle in 707. In Beverley Minster lies the tomb of an Earl Percy, slain by his own tenants in riots at Topcliffe in 1489. In the Church of St. Dennis, York, lies another Earl Percy of Northumberland who perished at Towton Field, while in the churchyard of Saxton near Towton, rests Lord Dacre, slain in the same battle and buried along with his charger, the skull of which was nu-earthed some four hundred years later. At St. Crux, York, is another of the Northumberlands, "executed upon the pavement" at the foot of the Market Place for his part in the Battle of Bramham Moor. On Micklegate Bar one may well imagine the heads of the Duke of York, slain at the Battle of Wakefield, or of Robert Aske, "captain" of the Pilgrimage of Grace, placed along with half a hundred other such gory remains to dry and shrivel in the sun.

At Newbald, East Yorkshire, hangs an enchanting monument to Sir Phillip Monckton, a hero of the Civil Wars, and at Knaresborough, heavy with heraldry, lie the tombs of

Tombs of Battle Heroes

Above: Lord Dacre was killed at the Battle of Towton and buried in this tomb in Saxton churchyard. The skull of his charger was unearthed some four hundred years later.

Opposite page, top: Bilbrough church, three miles from Marston Moor, contains the grey altar tomb of "Black Tom" Fairfax. (Photo by permission of the Vicar of Bilbrough).

Opposite page, bottom: The Slingsby Chapel at Knaresborough parish church has some fine heraldry, and is an excellent example of a military chapel. (Photo by permission of the Vicar of Knaresborough).

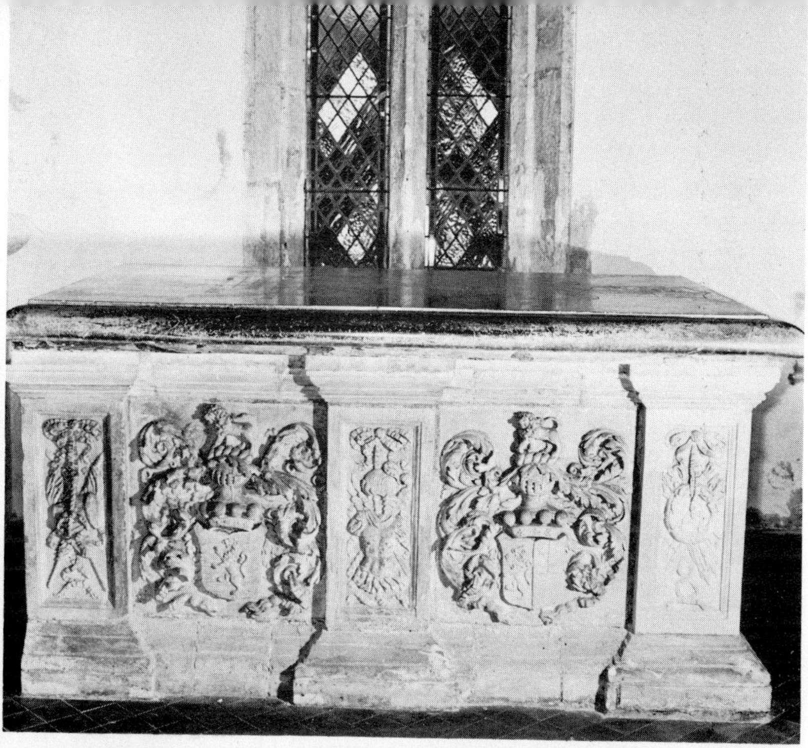

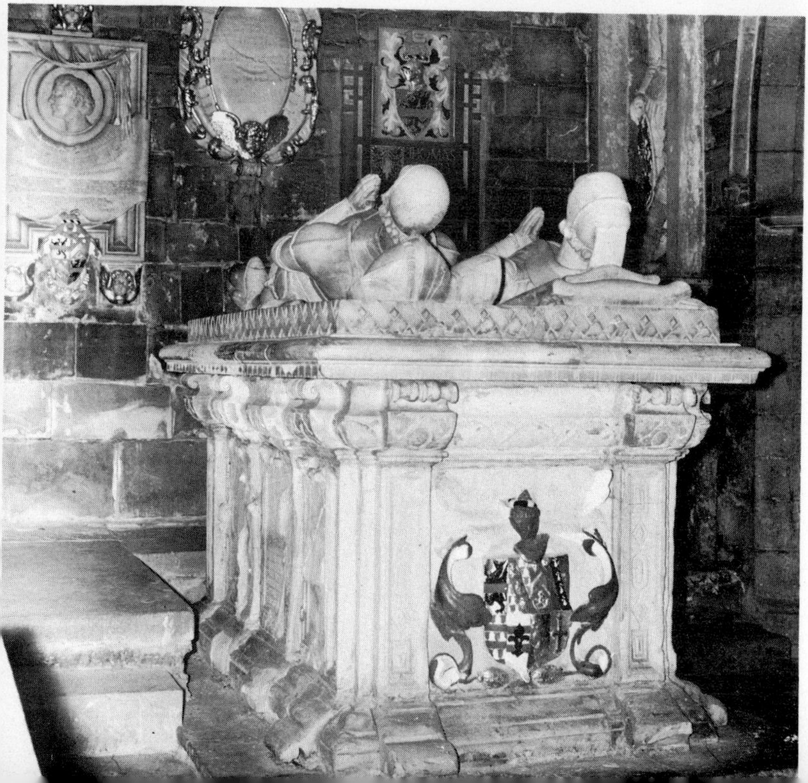

the Yorkshire soldiering family of Slingsby. In Ripley one can discover the lovely chapel of the Ingilbys, while at Boynton are monuments to the Strickland family. During the Civil Wars one member of this family hid the Queen of England, who departed carrying with her into Holland the Strickland family plate as a non-returnable "loan". At Ryther, near Tadcaster, are the tombs of the fighting Rythers, and at Stillingfleet hangs an oak door on which "mony an old Dane's skin has been nailed on th' one 'at went afore it." There are other monuments in Yorkshire, such as those of the Bellasis family of Coxwold, the tombs of the warring Marmions of Tanfield and the Markenfield tomb at Ripon. In the church of Bolton Percy are the Fairfax monuments, while at Bilbrough, three miles from the scene of his historic charges on Marston Moor, is the old grey altar tomb of "Black Tom" Fairfax, beloved by countless Yorkshiremen.

Emerging from the quiet of old churches, one can turn again to ancient battlefields and behold once more the waving grasses of Moor Lane on Marston Moor or the planking of a wooden bridge at Cocksford, still seeming to echo the shouts of Towton Field. Above Winwoed, Saxon battlefield of fifteen hundred years ago, the lights of modern Leeds spring up as night falls down. Twenty miles distant on the banks of the flowing Swale, the lamps of cottages shine beside Myton village, or dawn breaks above the towers of York, the weed-sluiced stream of Stamford Bridge, the camp of the Danes at Riccall or the lonely old hill of Sandal, Wakefield. It is in turning from such scenes that one may hope to tell more fully, not only the stories of Yorkshire battles but of the men who fought and died in them.

2:

From Roman Times to the Norman Conquest

MANY historians will agree that the most important Celtic or British tribe at the time of the Roman invasions of Britain almost 2,000 years ago was that of the Brigantes, who in those days occupied most of northern Britain including what is today called Yorkshire. They were the most powerful, warlike and best-informed people of this island, their capital city being Isuer Brigantum, later to become known to the Romans as Isurium. Built into an angle of the Yorkshire rivers, Tut and Ure, it is known today as Aldborough near Boroughbridge. In the Grasswoods above Grassington in Wharfedale, as well as many miles further northwards at Stanwick near Richmond, there existed other considerable fortresses which some historians have claimed as having been of even greater military importance than Isuer Brigantum.

It was in B.C. 55 that the Romans, premier race of the then known world, first entered Britain. At that time they did not stay very long, their invasion being of a purely explorative nature. Not until A.D. 43 did some 40,000 Roman legionaries commanded by one Aulus Plautius, later to be assisted by the Roman Emperor Claudius, return to this island, when the task of subduing the Celts or Britons commenced in earnest.

Apart from the many Celtic tribes known by different names from end to end of Britain, there existed in addition to the Yorkshire Brigantes, two other peoples as unwilling as were the Brigantes themselves to submit to Roman rule. They were the Silures and Ordovices, later to become known as the Welsh. Prince of the Silures was Caractacus or Caradoc, and it was this valiant chieftain who bravely resisted the Romans. Despite the assistance of one Venutius, divorced husband of Queen Cartesmandhua of the Brigantes, he was defeated in battle and had little option but to flee to the Brigantine Court of Isuer Brigantum. Here the vicious Queen Cartesmandhua, at war with her own divorced husband, pressed by enemies and desirous only of preserving her own magnificence, betrayed Caractacus to Rome. Had the Britons in general at this stage united their forces instead of each tribe attempting to fight its own battles, the Romans might never have penetrated the north at all. As it was, with Caractacus carried in chains to Rome, Venutius, now alone and having striven for years against the ever-encroaching legions, was forced into submission. Thus it happened that from the year A.D. 70 onwards few sounds were to be heard in the Celtic north save the tramp of these Roman armies.

Between the fastnesses of the mountain forests to the east and west of the impassable fenland of Yorkshire's southern rivers, there ran but a single track of land. It was to either side of this highway—which some have claimed as a part of Ermine Street— and north of the river Don that the Brigantes built lines of entrenchments still recognisable around such districts as Barwick near Leeds. Many battles were fought in this region, but northwards and still northwards rolled the Roman legions. With the fall of Doncaster—The Caer Dune of the Celts and the Danum of the Romans—the first line of British defence was in a state of surrender. Defeat of the second line along the banks of Aire and Calder became a foregone conclusion. With Roman eagles flaunting above Castleford—the Legeoleum of the Romans—and making use of a still-existent highway, the legions were in the Elmet country. Here the Britons offered a final resistance, having raised many earthworks or added to some already there above the Cock Beck beside Barwick, Becca and Aberford. Many battles are reputed to have been fought before the legions, tramping northwards, left this part of Yorkshire mainly in Roman hands. Under the rule of the Romans, the northern Brigantes—much as they may have detested Roman ways—learned Latin culture. They also lost the will to fight. Under such circumstances the recall of the Romans about the year 410 left the British people, particularly in Yorkshire, an easy prey to far more threatening invaders.

The Battle of Hatfield or Heathfield, Doncaster, A.D. 633.

IT was almost immediately following the departure of the Romans that there invaded the north—as indeed most of Britain—a people composed of Saxons, Angles and Jutes, later to become known as Anglo-Saxons. It would appear that as early as the first century they had been dwelling in lands on either side of the European Elbe estuary and in Schleswig. During the migrations which had upset Europe from the third to the fifth century, they had travelled westwards, some to Frisia and some to the Lower Rhine, while others had taken to raiding or settling on the coasts of present day Yorkshire. It has been claimed that many of these fighting people were first brought into Britain about the year 445 by Vortigern, a Celtic over-king, to be used as mercenaries against the northern Picts. Led by the celebrated chieftains, Hengist and Horsa, these armies first defeated Vortigern's enemies, then Vortigern in person, and finally sent for their friends and families to settle on English shores. All these invaders were of much the same stock, speaking approximately the same language. Most of their kings claimed descent from Odin or Wodin, an ancient sovereign magnified by superstition into a god. Being pagan and professing a bloodier and to them far more satisfying religion than the Christianity of the Britons, they not only detested this faith but were prepared to fight it to the death. Armed with spears, axes, swords of tempered steel, and spiked sledge hammers probably copied from the Hammer of Thor, they must have been grim opponents for the peaceful northern Britons who were Roman armed but lacked any form of Roman cohesion. During several centuries, battle after battle swept the north, doing little to unite the British and Saxon races.

Yet by the commencement of the seventh century, there had arrived at least a partial settlement of the north in the founding of the Saxon Celtic states of Bernicia, between Tyne and Tees, and Deira, between Tees and Humber. Both districts were to receive in 617 the title of Northumbria. Among the ensuing kings of this vast area—still a region of forests and rushing rivers—was a certain Edwin, who by success in war and politics managed to raise the north of England to a superiority transcending all the rest of Britain. King Edwin, after leaning towards the paganism of the Saxon, was converted to the Christianity of Britain, partly through the teachings of the celebrated Roman missionary Paulinus, and partly by his marriage to Ethelburga, Christian princess of Kent. One example of the work of Paulinus in Northumbria was the baptising of no less than 12,000 northern Christian converts in the river Swale at Topcliffe, near Thirsk.

Following his Christian conversion, King Edwin became so powerful that in 633 one Penda, heathen ruler of nearby Mercia and antagonistic towards all Christians, combined with Cadwallada, King of North Wales, to attack Edwin at Hatfield or Heathfield, near Doncaster. A terrible fight took place. At the very commencement of this sanguinary battle, Edwin's favourite son, Offred, was pierced by an arrow and fell dead at his father's feet. The king, side by side with his friend and ally, King Godbald of the Orkneys, rushed into the heart of the conflict and was himself slain at the feet of his hated enemy. Edwin's armies fled in all directions, and so great was the animosity of King Penda that both he and the Welsh king, Cadwallada, perpetrated the most frightful slaughter. In extending this to old men, children, women and monks, they left their names to be damned for ever throughout the north. The future of Northumbria now seemed so black that even the great Paulinus, carrying with him Ethelburga, the King's widowed Queen, took ship for Kent. He was received by the weeping king of that country, and never returned to the north.

The decapitated head of King Edwin was carried secretly to York and buried in the chapel of St. Gregory, which the King had been engaged in building. Forty-eight years of age at the time of his death, Edwin had ruled Northumbria with the greatest honour for 17 years, and so great had been his zeal for the Christian faith that it obtained him a place in the Calendar of the English church. Prince Oswald, his successor, in bidding fair to become as great a ruler as his uncle, fell upon King Cadwallada near Hexham, and not only defeated his armies but killed this "detestable heathenish so-called invincible." As a result the conversion of Northumbria to the Christian faith was brought forward, but the life of King Oswald, was destined to be of short duration for he was slain by his ancient enemy, King Penda.

For those who might wish to make some exploration of the battlefield of Hatfield, it lies some seven miles north-east of Doncaster and three miles south-west of Stainforth or "paved ford" across which the armies of King Edwin are believed to have entered the battle. A short distance from the village of Hatfield is a place known as "The Lings," where the battle is believed to have been fought, while east of the Hatfield road still remains Slay Pits Lane leading to Slay Pits. Apart from these small clues, together with a few supposed relics of the battle preserved in Hatfield church, little survives today of a battlefield which altered the story of the north.

The Battle of Winwoed, Wynwood or Whinney Moor, A.D. 655.

IT was twenty years after the Battle of Hatfield that nemesis overtook King Penda. Detested by thousands and having recently desolated East Anglia, he advanced into Northumbria, his armies swelled by thirty vassal kings—Welsh and Cumbrian as well as Saxon. Sworn to exterminate the Christian

Modern flats tower above a 7th century battlefield. Grime's Dyke at Seacroft marks the generally accepted site of the Battle of Winwoed, which on November 15th, 665, saw the defeat of the Mercian ruler, King Penda.

faith, Penda had never been able to forsake his heathen gods. Pagan to the last with a consistency worthy of a better cause, he "despised those who he saw not doing the works of their faith."

For the sake of his subjects, and wishing to abstain from conflict, King Oswy offered Penda many gifts of gold and silver but in vain. One desire only had Penda, the annihilation of his foes, and he came to a place near "Loidis-in-Elmet," known today as Leeds, and to a moor beside Barwick—the generally accepted battlefield of Winwoed, Wynwood or Whinney Moor.

The Battle of Winwoed was fought on November 15th, 655, and in ferocity equalled any battle ever waged in England. This fight was well-matched. King Penda's principal ally,

23

Ethelbald, a rebel nephew of King Oswy, retired for a while in order to see how the battle fared and then withdrew his forces from the field. Thus by late afternoon Penda lacked the assistance he required, and not only he but every one of his thirty generals was slain. Apart from thousands of warriors killed on the field, thousands more were drowned in the flooding Cock Beck where it runs beside the village of Barwick-in-Elmet, or in the not far distant river Aire. With the end of Penda the cause of the heathen gods was lost for ever. The gratitude of King Oswy for his unexpected victory was such that no less than twelve great abbeys were built across the north, and the King not only dedicated his young daughter to the Church but himself took her to the Lady Hilda. She afterwards moved with her nuns from Hartlepool to Whitby, where there soon arose one of the most splendid abbeys on the coast.

There can be little doubt of the whereabouts of the battle-field of Winwoed. Situated in the once great fighting country of both Celt and Saxon, and a little to the south of the present day Leeds to Tadcaster highway beyond Seacroft, an incline still runs downhill towards Grime's Dyke and Grime's Dyke Farm. It was on the Seacroft side of this stream where the Cock Beck runs down towards Becca Banks that the battle was fought. Among many strange stories of this ancient district, none can be more strange than a legend which has long been carried forward through an old rhyme quoted by local residents until recently. It tells how, at death, the soul in a kind of probational journey must pass the wastes of "Whinney Moor":

> If hosen and shoon thou never gave none
> Every neght and awle
> The whins shall prick thee to the bare bone
> And Christe receive thy sawle.

> If ever thou gave either meate or drinke
> Every neght and awle
> The fire shall never make thee shrinke
> And Christe receive thy sawle.

The Danes and the Battle of Brunanberg, A.D. 937.

FOLLOWING the Battles of Hatfield and Winwoed a new way of life was born into England. It set aside the thought that war was the beginning and end of human existance and began to reach out, particularly in Northumbria, towards art and learning. Much has been written on the works of King Oswy following his defeat of Penda, and of men such as Bishop Theodore, St. Chad of York, St. Wilfrid of Ripon and many others, as well as on the building of schools and the growing interest in the study of manuscript works. With the mass of Anglo-Saxon peoples still accepting Christianity as a kind of magic, many old pagan customs such as the keeping of Yule were lending colour to their lives. The coming of such mighty personalities as Caedmon, the poet of Whitby, Bede of Jarrow, the famous Saint Hilda and Alfried of Northumbria, created an influence which even today embellishes the world of letters.

Unfortunately at this moment all such development in the north, as well as over most of Europe, was arrested by the upsurge of the Danes. As fearless sailors and splendid ship-wrights, these naturally warlike people had formerly estab-lished themselves as merchants, but during the latter part of the eighth century had turned to piracy. It was during 793 that they first robbed and burned the monastic settlements of the sacred isle of Lindisfarne and then the beautiful church of Jarrow. The people of bygone Yorkshire frequently wit-nessed the arrival of these terrible Danish ships of war, alive from stem to stern with armed men and with war shields hanging at the prows of every vessel. It must have been agon-ising for the now peaceful Saxons to watch the vessels dropping anchor beside what today are known as Whitby, Scarborough, Bridlington or Spurn. By 867 the Danes had taken York. It was into this picture there came at last one of the most famous of English kings, Alfred the Great, who gradually reduced the Danes—except in Northumbria—to a state of temporary submission. It was left for King Edward, son of Alfred, to complete his father's work and to break the power of the Danes in the north. Finally, it was Edward's son, King Athelstane, who defeated both Dane and Scot in the celebrated Battle of Brunanberg in 937.

At this time King Olaf, Danish pretender to the throne of Northumbria, had allied with King Constantine of Scotland and was aided by "many great armies" from the districts of Strathclyde, Cumbria and Wales. This force sailed in 650 warships along the Yorkshire shore of the river Humber, but despite the enormous array of ships and men King Athelstane gained a magnificent victory. Long before the fight was ended, no less than five Danish kings and seven earls lay dead upon the field. Such was King Athelstane's triumph at this famous yet in many ways obscure battle that, with his enemies fleeing in all directions, he was able to announce himself as King of the whole of England.

So great has been the controversy concerning Brunanberg that no less than thirty distinct places have been chosen by experts as the site of the struggle, these ranging from Burnswark in Dumfriesshire to Bourne in Lincolnshire. But a good deal of evidence points to the most likely site lying near Rotherham. Wherever the site may be, it is certain that Athelstane's victory brought to the English people, and again especially to the inhabitants of Northumbria, a feeling of greater security than had hitherto been known. Yet with the murder of King Edmund, brother and successor to Athelstane, and with the eventual succession of the foolish Saxon monarch, Ethelred the Unready, the Danes returned to England. At first this new invasion merely ravaged the coasts, but on meeting with little resistance its pagan leader, Sweyne, resolved to settle in the land. Fortunately Sweyne lived only a year or so, and then the reins of government fell to his son, Canute. Although a Dane, he became one of our greatest kings, but his death and the almost simultaneous deaths of his two sons gave the Witanagemot a major problem. On the approach of Sweyne, King Ethelred had fled to Normandy, and it was from here that the Government brought his son to become King Edward or "Edward the Confessor." This weak and senile old man was made the bane of Saxon England, but on his death Harold, son of the late King's adviser Earl Godwin, seized the throne in the face of a promise previously extracted from him. This was to the effect that on the death of the "Confessor" he would hand over the throne to Duke William of Normandy, an action which precipitated the Norman Conquest. The "curtain raiser" of this—although few people may have realised the fact—was the Battle of Stamford Bridge in Yorkshire.

The Battle of Stamford Bridge, A.D. 1066.

NO sooner had Harold possessed himself of the throne of England than news was brought to him, not only of the projected landing of a Norman army on England's southern coasts but of the landing in the Humber of 60,000 invading Danes and Norwegians. Led by Harald Hardrada, King of Norway, and accompanied by Tostig, rebel Earl of Northumbria and brother of the English king, this Scandinavian army soon showed its intentions of annexing at least the north of England. On hearing of this Danish landing two Saxon

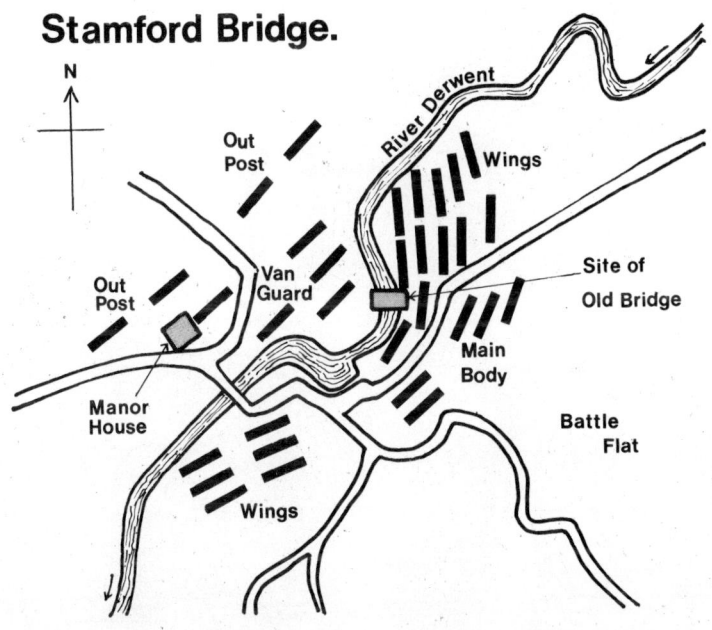

Plan of the Battle of Stamford Bridge.

earls, Edwin and Morcar, brothers-in-law of Harold of England, lost little time in marching from York towards the Scandinavian camp at Riccall, a few miles further down the river. No sooner had they reached the village of Fulford below the city than they were set upon by Hardrada's army and totally defeated. The terrified citizens of York handed over the keys of the city to the invaders.

Throughout the whole of the summer King Harold of England had been watching the southern coast, but now—giving up all thought of the Normans he united his forces and hurried north in one of the greatest forced marches in history. The Norwegian and Danish invaders, now re-assembled at Riccall and inebriated by their easy victory over Edwin and Morcar, had no notion of Harold's advance from the south and were completely surprised when a great English army

27

Men at War

Above: The rout of the English at Fulford, York, immediately prior to the Battle of Stamford Bridge. An army of 60,000 men led by Harald Hardrada, King of Norway, utterly defeated the army of the two Saxon earls, Edwin and Morcar.

Opposite: Stand of the Vikings at Stamford Bridge. A powerful Norwegian armed with a giant battle-axe reputedly killed 50 Englishmen before being dealt a death wound by a soldier who sailed down a stream in a swill-tub.

burst on them within a few days of their landing. Hardrada, closely followed by Harold, retreated eastwards and drew up his forces at Stamford Bridge straddling the river Derwent. Before offering battle King Harold is reputed to have sent twenty horsemen to parley with Earl Tostig.

"In the name of England," said these messengers, "we offer you the whole of Northumbria or if this be insufficient, a third part of all England if you will sail away."

"And what," demanded Tostig, "would King Harold give to Hardrada?"

"Seven feet of English earth for a grave," cried the English ambassadors, "or since he be a giant we might make it eight!"

And with that there took place such a battle as had rarely been seen. No quarter was asked or given; from seven in the morning until three in the afternoon the struggle raged with dreadful slaughter. At first the fight was on the west or further bank of the river and opposite to the present day village. The English army, charging downhill towards the narrow plain that still exists beside the stream, made a terrific onslaught on the Norwegian vanguard which, after a struggle, was driven backwards across the wooden bridge some distance above the stone bridge of today. Here a powerful Norwegian armed with a giant battle-axe had taken up his stand. In vain the English sought to dislodge this warrior from the bridge, and it is recorded that before he fell he had slain no less than fifty Englishmen. Struck by whole flights of arrows, the missiles refused to penetrate his armour. Only when an English soldier entered a swill-tub and sailed down the stream to deal him a death wound through the planking of the bridge, did the Norwegian splash into the torrent. Their hero dead, the Norwegians yielded the bridge and fell back on their main body. On this the English army swarmed, sword in hand, not only across the bridge but across the flowing river, "the living walking upon the dead whose bodies locked the stream." Little by little the Norwegians were dislodged from the ground which rises on the east bank of the river until both hill and village were carried. Here the Norwegians made their final stand, a pitched battle took place ending only in the complete defeat of the Norwegian host.

Although the losses on the English side were great, those among the Norwegians were incredible. Thousands died on the field, thousands of others were drowned in the rushing river, and many more died on their ships at Riccall to which their army had retreated. Among the dead were both Hardrada and Tostig, King Harold slaying his brother Tostig with his

The ironwork on the Old Dane's door at Stillingfleet parish church, near Selby, is said to commemorate the Battle of Stamford Bridge. Almost as fascinating is the magnificent carved stonework.

own sword. So terrible was the plight of the Norwegian fugitives that out of some 500 ships which were claimed to have brought them to England, only twenty were needed to carry them home. Of the dead, most were either thrown into deep pits or left by the villagers to moulder on the field. Meanwhile, with King Harold and his armies feasting in York, there came swift messengers to inform him that during his absence from the south, William the Norman had landed near Pevensey. Harold of England, hurrying southwards, was himself to meet death at the Battle of Hastings, October 14th 1066, while William the Norman became William the Conqueror.

The battlefield of Stamford Bridge has few remains to be seen. The village lies eight miles north-east of York on the Driffield road, and is divided into two unequal parts. On the west bank of the Derwent, on which at the time of the battle lay the vanguard of the invading army, there still remains a tract of level ground rising to a slope down which the English charged. On the village side of the river, above the rising crest, is Battle Flats, but few relics have been uncovered since the eighteenth century. A field at the northern end of the village is still called "Dane's Garth."

3:   *Through the Middle Ages*

THE Conqueror showed himself a despot from the very first moment of the Conquest, when the Normans—delirious with victory—paraded their horses among the Saxon dead of Hastings. Acre by acre he first overthrew England's south-eastern coasts and counties, and then reached northwards to slay the warriors of Surrey, Sussex and Hampshire before proceeding into Hertfordshire, where he established a camp at Berkhamsted to cut off the warlike north. The great Saxon earls, Edwin and Morcar, retreated into Yorkshire, recruiting the fighters of the Midlands as they passed. At Christmas, 1066, the Conqueror was crowned King of England at Westminster by Aldred, Archbishop of York, who was the only English prelate willing to undertake the task and then "only in the name of peace." For a while the Norman king seemed willing to placate his Saxon subjects, but about March 1067 the rapaciousness of his Norman followers caused him to enlarge his conquests.

It was due to this attitude, and to the growing menace of the Norman baronage in the north, that Yorkshiremen began to show their teeth. William withdrew into Normandy, an event which many historians claim was a direct incitement to Saxon uprisings so that the conquest might be further prosecuted. In any event rebellion flared like a beacon. By 1086 war had spilled across most of England and the whole of the north was in a ferment. In Yorkshire bands of outlaws drawn from the persecuted Saxon nobility were taking oath that none should sleep beneath a roof until the Normans were driven out of England. Hearing of these things—or having awaited such news—William returned to England and marched northwards, meeting Edwin and Morcar "where Ouse and Humber conjoin." He inflicted such a bloody defeat that thousands of Saxons fled for the hills or for the supposed safety of York, although this city was soon surrounded and eventually both subdued and garrisoned by the troops of the Conqueror. The Normans, aided by the labour of thousands of Saxons, now set about delving, building and fortifying in order that York might become the premier fortress of the north.

Northumbrian and Yorkshire chieftains, such as Prince Merleysweyn, Earl Gospatric, Gospatric de Rigton, "cousin of the earl," and the sons of Earl Siward and Archil, fled into Scotland. The Normans themselves did not have an easy time. William Mallet, the newly appointed Norman Governor of York, was soon making it clear to the Conqueror that the country around the city, later known as the Ainstie, and the Forest of Galtres, was becoming precariously dangerous. Robert de Comine, a Norman commander with more conceit than military capability, marched northwards through Yorkshire with the intention of conquering County Durham, and was set on by Saxon guerillas while debauching in Durham City. He was burned alive in his lodgings together with most of his military staff.

At the time of their attack on Durham, the Saxons had long been expecting powerful allies from abroad, and these soon began to arrive. Many of them were sons of Danish warriors whose relatives—after fighting under King Canute—had settled in England and now asked for assistance from their kinsfolk. At the same time the Court of Denmark was being besieged by Saxon chieftains, begging the Danish king to lend a hand in the re-conquest of the north, while Saxon nobles who had fled into Scotland were doing all in their power to enlist the help of the Scottish king. It was into the midst of these preparations that King Sweyne of Denmark suddenly despatched to England a fleet of some 340 vessels carrying armies of Poles, Saxons, Scots, Norwegians, Danes and martial adventurers of every sort. On hearing of the arrival of these foreign levies, thousands of Dalesmen forsook the fastness of the uplands and came hurrying to join them. With York well-known to many of the Saxon nobles now returned from Scotland, it was decided to encircle and take the city. William Mallet, the Governor, set fire to some houses so that his assailants could not use the materials for filling up the ditch, but unfortunately fired the town in the process. Flames wafted in all directions and men and women fled for their lives. No less than 3,000 Normans, preferring death in battle to burning alive, issued from the city and were promptly put to slaughter. York Minster and its priceless library was burned to the ground, while Mallet only saved his life and those of his family by going on board a Danish vessel for eventual ransom.

As a result of this Saxon insurrection, there came to the north of England a vengeance such as few nations can ever have experienced.

The Harrying of the North,

NEWS of the Saxon rebellion reached the Conqueror while he was hunting in the Forest of Dean. Even his personal friends had shrunk in terror. "Per Deum Splendorum—By the Splendour of God!" roared William, at the same time swearing that not a rood of northern land, a cottage or a human life should go unscathed. William crossed the river Aire, bribed the Danes who turned forthwith to brigandry, and then staked out his "claim of death". Village after village, as becomes apparent from the pages of Domesday Book, met its blackened end, and appalled by such savagery the Saxon leaders again fled into Scotland never to return. Among all these leaders the only one who remained to face the Conqueror was Gospatric de Rigton—the ditch of his manor house is claimed by some to remain to this day behind Rigton schoolhouse. So great was the Norman vengeance that 100,000 persons died among the snowy fields of Yorkshire, and "for twelve long years the land lay barren whilst towns stood stark for half a century."

King William's commissioners then came with sword in hand to lay the foundations of a new Norman aristocracy, although they did not always discriminate between gold and jewels due to the King or to be abstracted for themselves. These so-called aristocrats, who were in reality little more than robbers, included William de Percy, ancestor of the Earls of Northumberland, who was given eighty Saxon manors. Vast tracts of land in North Yorkshire fell into the hands of Alan the Red who, as cousin to the Conqueror, built the still-existent castle of Richmond besides the rushing Swale. At the same time Ilbert de Lacy constructed Pontefract Castle, William de Warrenne much of the earlier portion of Sandal, and De Busli the castle of Tickhill. From end to end of Yorkshire lay the mighty shadow of the De Mowbrays, and soon there would arrive the powerful Houses of Clifford of Skipton and Scrope of Wensleydale. Added to these were many lesser Norman names such as Vavasour of Hazlewood, while other familes of Saxon origin—some representing the blood royal of England—fled into the higher dales and may be traced today among simple sheep farming families as old as Yorkshire. From the Saxon leaders who escaped to Scotland leaving their tenants to fend as best they might, many nobles, were destined to come down through the centuries in the Scottish and border earldoms of Neville, Lennox and Dunbar.

The Battle of the Standard, 1138.

WHEN King Henry I, son of the Conqueror, lost his only son, Prince William, in the wreck of the *White Ship* on it's voyage across the Channel in 1120, he also lost the direct male heir to England. Deprived of this heir, King Henry did all in his power to ensure the throne for his daughter, Matilda. But on his death the nobles of England, and especially of Yorkshire, entirely disregarded their promises of support for the Princess Matilda, and voted the throne to Stephen, Count of Blois, a nephew of the late king. This brave and capable soldier was so foolishly over-generous as to bring the country to ruin. Among King Stephen's greatest enemies was his own cousin, Robert Earl of Gloucester, the late king's illegitimate son. After pretending to have become reconciled with Stephen, he took an oath of fealty by which he was able to obtain possession of his own estates in England, and then set about promoting the cause of his half-sister, Matilda. Under such betrayals the extravagant and inconsequent reign of Stephen soon fell on evil times.

Gloucester, having made plans for a great rebellion, first obtained a promise of support from King David of Scotland, Matilda's uncle, and then fled abroad. At the same time many English barons accused Stephen—who had by this time squandered most of his funds—of having failed them financially, and withdrew in dudgeon to their castles. News was then suddenly brought to Stephen to the effect that David of Scotland, keeping his word to Gloucester and Matilda, had crossed the Scottish border, accompanied by his son, Prince Henry. They intended "like Scotch ants to overrun the country 'twixt Tweed and Tees." Mild and merciful as the Scottish king was reputed to be, his followers showed every shade of barbarity and spared neither age, sex or even the unborn child. Ever since Saxon times hatred had existed between the Scottish and English peoples and, in facing King David's invasion, Stephen's generals made ample use of this fact in order to raise the ire of their Saxon soldiers. Out of the crypts of ancient churches were dragged the Saxon banners of St. John of Beverley, St. Cuthbert of Durham, St. Peter of York and St. Wilfrid of Ripon.

So rapid was the advance of the Scots that Stephen, unable to reach the scene in time, delegated the command of the

Anglo-Norman army to Thurston, Archbishop of York, an infirm old man but one whose warlike energies were not impaired by disease or illness. As though exhorted by some heavenly agency, the Archbishop lost little time in calling on all Englishmen—Saxon or Norman—to fight to the last, and promised on behalf of the Church the immediate acceptance by heaven of all who should fall in battle with the Scots. From all over came yeomen and farmlads led by their parish priests, "the bravest men in Yorkshire." Although sickness prevented the Archbishop from attending in person, he appointed the Bishop of Durham to represent him on the field, and at the same time handed the more energetic commands to William Peverell and Walter Espec of Nottinghamshire and Gilbert de Lacy of Yorkshire. Since the Scottish armies had already passed the Tees, the Anglo-Norman commanders drew up between that river and the Humber at a place called Elfertun—today known as Northallerton.

Here the priests erected a remarkable standard—a cart to which was fastened a tall mast surmounted by a silver pyx or box containing a holy wafer and flanked by streamers bearing the emblems of the saints. Around this standard—hence the Battle of the Standard—were grouped the picked men of Yorkshire, Nottinghamshire and Lincolnshire, "strong Saxons armed with bows and arrows two cubits in length" to whom the Normans gladly conceded the forefront of the fight. The Scots, whose standard was merely a bunch of heather, had crossed the Tees by divisions. The first, commanded by Prince Henry, consisted of pikemen from the Lowlands, archers from Teviotdale and Liddesdale, troopers from Cumberland and Westmorland, and fierce, half-naked men of Galloway who wore no armour but insisted on leading the battle. Next came the Highland clans, the small targ and broadsword or claymore being their only weapon. Behind all these rode the King himself surrounded by guards of both English and Scottish origin. These Scottish armies marched through the mists to the undulating slope some three miles north of Northallerton, marked today by an obelisk on which appears in bronze relief a picture of the chariot.

Two Norman knights, Balliol and Bruce, who had rich lands in England and had deserted the Scottish armies, informed the English of the arrival of the Scots. At first the terrible onslaught of the naked Gallwegians broke through the English ranks with such ferocity that the battle was almost won. The Norman horse however rallied round the standard, and made charge after charge on the maddened Scotsmen.

The Saxon bowmen then took up positions on both wings of their own army and harassed the Scots with a murderous discharge of arrows, while the Norman men-at-arms received the Gallwegians on their lances. Against the armour of the Normans the long, thin pikes of the men of Galloway shivered to splinters. Even so the Highlanders, shouting "Alban! Alban!", kept on attempting to cut their way through this mass of ironclad cavalry. It was the first time the Normans had come into contact with the northern broadsword and many a warrior had cause to remember the experience. For two full hours the Scots, often completely unarmed, continued to fight a now hopelessly unequal contest, with Prince Henry penetrating almost to the standard.

As in the case of many a similar battle the end was sudden, the Scottish armies becoming panic-stricken and fleeing in all directions. With their King doing all in his power to stem the flight, and in some cases causing a brief yet impossible respite to this bloody ending, most of the Scottish army never ceased fleeing until it reached Carlisle. Of the Scottish contingents no less than 12,000 lay dead on the field, while the Anglo-Normans were not in a state to continue the chase. Nevertheless, the Battle of the Standard—if it accomplished little else—did at least lead to a better understanding. King Stephen's queen, who was a Saxon princess and niece of King David, held an interview with her uncle in Durham city. Stephen agreed to leave the English counties of Cumberland and Westmorland in Scottish hands and, having invested Prince Henry with the Earldom of Northumberland, might have led his own kingdom to stability. But in an evil moment he aroused not only his barons but, what was of greater portent, the anger of the Church Militant of his day and age.

For the traveller who might wish to discover the battlefield of the Standard, it may be best in the first place to enter Northallerton. At the northern end of the town the left hand highway towards Darlington leads a straight three miles to the Standard Field, a soft undulating slope on which a very few relics have been discovered during the last two centuries.

The White Battle of Myton-on-Swale, 1319.

HENRY II, cousin of King Stephen and son of the Countess Matilda, ascended the throne on the death of Stephen, and proved to be a splendid king. He was followed by Richard I—better known as Coeur de Lion—and then by the vicious King John, but neither of these monarchs had been able to undo the work of King Henry. Even on the accession of that utterly futile ruler, Henry III, son of King John, little harm had been done to England. With the coming of Edward I, however, there fell on the country, through no fault of the King, battle after battle concerning the Scottish succession. In passing from life at the head of his armies beside the Solway Firth, this splendid soldier, so long known as "Hammer of the Scots," must surely have mourned on account of the poltroon son whom he would leave behind him. Few if any historians have spoken or written well of King Edward II. Led throughout his earlier years by his handsome, dissolute favourite, Piers Gaveston, this brainless monarch had lacked even the good sense to hide his grimaces when his appalling favourite had squandered both wit and insulting nicknames on the greatest persons in the land. To the great Earl of Lincoln the twain had jointly appended the title "Brostebelly," and to the Earl of Warwick "the Black Dog of Ardenne."

"Let me but lay my hands upon Gaveston," had whispered Warwick, "he shall feel the black dog's teeth!" With the absence of the King from England, Gaveston had been appointed Regent and upset almost everybody in the land. As a result he was snatched by certain of the nobles out of Scarborough Castle and clandestinely beheaded. Rabid with anger, the king swore on his return that he would never rest until the murderers had paid for the killing with their lives. Matters in England, however, now went from bad to worse with the King's vacillating policies ending in the crushing defeat of the English armies at Bannockburn. Scottish armies trooped into England and, with raiding and burning in all directions, there came to Yorkshire that so called "White Battle" of Myton destined to send the hate between the two nations galloping down the centuries.

The battlefield of Myton lies three miles east of the town of Boroughbridge, not far from the quiet village of Myton and just above the confluence of the rivers Swale and Ure. It was in 1319 that Edward II, while attempting to wipe out the disgrace of Bannockburn in the besieging of Berwick, heard that the Scottish lords, Douglas and Randolph, were intent on creating a diversion. They had marched into England where, having first collected an army of some 15,000 men, they had crossed the Solway to embark on a campaign of havoc, rape and murder. Passing through the northern counties and entering Yorkshire, spoiling and burning as they went, they reached the town of Boroughbridge and reduced the place to ashes. Following this story of wanton destruction, they pushed on

39

The Battle of Boroughbridge, 1422

(see pages 44-48).

towards York. Hearing that Queen Isabella of England was lodging in the suburbs of the city, the Scottish lords had devised a plan to seize the Queen and hold her as hostage for any terms they might care to ask.

Esconced in York were Archbishop Melton, one of the so-called "fighting Meltons," John Hotham, Bishop of Ely and Chancellor of England, and the Abbot of Selby. They appear to have persuaded Sir Nicholas Flemming, Lord Mayor of York, to raise an army of noblemen, citizens, monks, priests and beggars in order to go out and rescue the Queen. Having effected this, and no doubt vastly elated by their prowess, they had sent off the Queen to Nottingham. Archbishop Melton, having had time to consider the evils of the Scots who had howled out insulting epithets beneath his walls, determined to set off in pursuit of the raiders. Pressing into service all who could travel, including peasants for miles around the city, Melton now set forth accompanied by a rabble composed of some 10,000 men. Scarcely any of them were soldiers, and many were simply monks and choristers from the stalls of the Cathedral. Hearing of the whereabouts of the Scottish armies, which consisted entirely of trained soldiers of Robert Bruce, the Yorkshiremen made their way along the eastern bank of the Ouse and Swale "walking stealthily that they might the better pounce upon their enemies." They finally discovered their enemy beside the village of Myton-on-Swale.

The Scots, fully apprised of the advance of the Yorkshire-men, awaited their arrival from behind some burning hayricks. Here the river Swale is crossed today by what was, until fifty years ago, a strong iron bridge of ornamental design. About a hundred yards below this bridge tradition speaks of an older structure of stone and wood, close to Myton Meadows which lie between the junction of the rivers Swale and Ure.

During the Battle of Myton Meadows—if battle it can be termed—the Scots first gave way to many blood-curdling yells and then sallied forth in two separate wings, "shielded shape," between the English and the bridge. Facing the terrible aspect of their Scottish foes, the armies of the Archbishop might well have retraced their steps to York had they been able to do so. As it was they were herded by the Scotsmen, inebriated by the sheer lust of killing, into a corner between the two rivers, and few dared to put up any fight at all. Driven yard by yard into the river, many were carried away in the torrent while hundreds of others lay dead on the field surrounded by the flaming stacks. Chief among these were over two hundred

The river Swale (foreground) joins the river Ure at Myton, scene of a terrible massacre in 1319. Raiding Scots drove the rabble army of Archbishop Melton of York into the triangle of land shown on the right of this view, which proved the most dreadful of death-traps. Men forced into the rivers were unable to escape owing to the steep banks.

monks with their white habits steeped in blood, hence the "white battle of Myton."

The rabid Scotsmen, returning to their senses and seeming at last to realise the horror of their deed, first stared in a terrified manner on the heaps of dead and then fled from the field. Realising that in their return northwards they might fall in with an English army, the Scottish leaders first hurried southwards towards Brotherton in order to reach the banks of the Aire and then turned homewards by way of the dales of Aire, Wharfe and Nidd, burning the churches and villages as they passed. The Archbishop and his immediate friends, possessed of fast horses, made what speed they might towards York. As night came down on the field of Myton, only the moon regarded the sightless dead.

Throughout the centuries many legends have been told concerning this stricken field, perhaps the most interesting being that of how a lonely countryman saw a glint in a nearby hedge and uncovered the Archbishop's gilded crozier, to return it to the Minster only when he felt a curse on him. As for the

43

people of York, never had there been such a city of mourning; never such hoardes of women and children trudging northwards in order to seek their dead. Most distinguished of these Myton dead was Sir Nicholas Flemming, whose body was carried home to be buried in the parish church of St. Wilfrid. Of the slain Lord Mayor it is stated that he had seven times filled the office of Mayor and that a chantry was raised to his memory in the church of his sepulchre—a church no longer in existence. Of York Minster it is said that so great had been its denudation of officials that for upwards of fifty years many of its stalls stood empty.

Myton Meadows are difficult to find. Approaching the site from Myton-on-Swale one crosses the old iron bridge below which the Swale runs down towards the battlefield. Almost two hundred yards below the bridge still lie one or two old stones which probably formed a part of the original bridge, but the road to the battlefield from a little lower down is more or less barred. The battlefield may also be approached by the Ure from Boroughbridge or by the left hand bank of the Swale downstream from Myton. One can easily understand the loss of so many men by drowning in either the battles of Myton or Boroughbridge.

The Battle of Boroughbridge, 1322.

EDWARD II was in dire disgrace with the people after the defeat of Myton. The time appeared opportune for Thomas Earl of Lancaster to attempt a government on his own account, but he proved to be little better as a ruler than the king and the country began to drift into anarchy. With the king harrying the Welsh borders, Lancaster and his supporters launched a major rebellion, but by February 1322 Edward had regained some semblance of popularity. On hearing that Lancaster was besieging the castle of Tickhill near Doncaster, he ordered the royal armies to move north. A short time later the Earl, having lost most of his stores in a flooded river near Burton-on-Trent, retreated to his own castle of Pontefract and would have been well advised to remain there. Instead of this he moved northwards and, while resting at Boroughbridge and making arrangements to cross the river Ure, received news that the king was also moving north towards the town.

Sir Andrew Harcla (or Harker), a knight of Wensleydale, left Ripon at the head of a large army of Cumbrians and intended to hold the Ure bridge for the king. Almost within

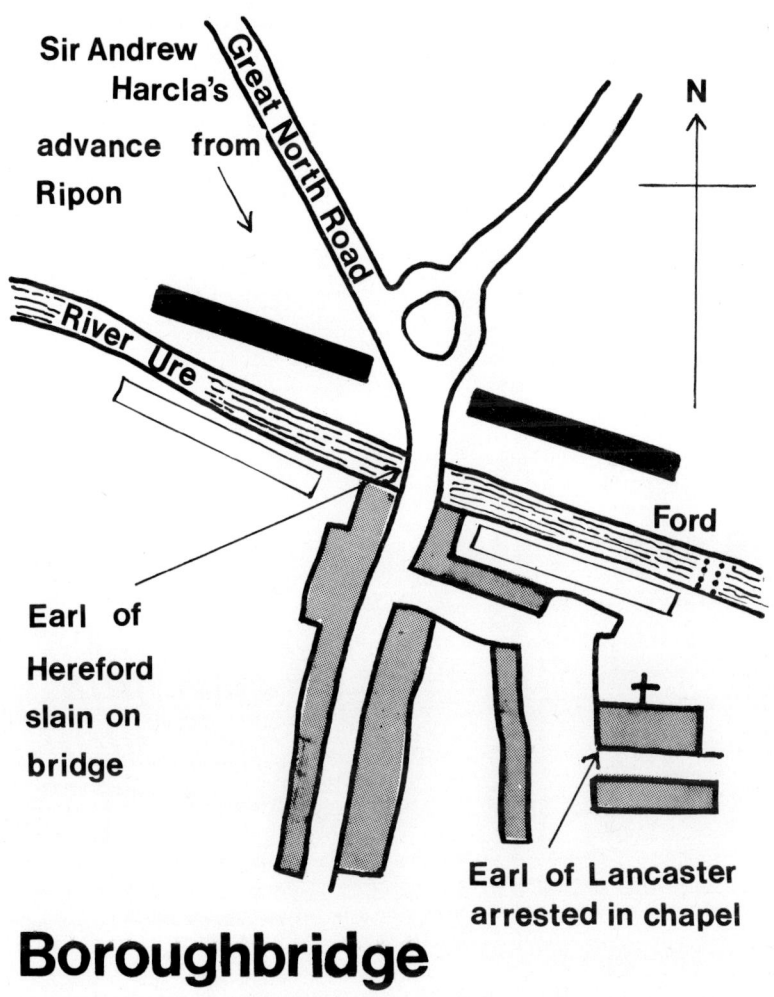

Plan of the Battle of Boroughbridge.

46

an hour the troops of Harcla appeared, lining the banks of the river opposite Boroughbridge and covering a line now occupied by the Ure Navigation canal. Lancaster and his confederate, the Earl of Hereford, discovered themselves likely to be penned in Boroughbridge, and attempted without success to intimidate Harcla on their own account. They then had no recourse but battle. Under these circumstances Lancaster's army, moving out of the town towards the bridge and occupying ground in the vicinity of the present day *Three Greyhounds* and *Crown* inns, made a gallant attempt to cross the river. Here Humphrey de Bohun, Lancaster's chief lieutenant, leading the mailed chivalry of England faced flight after flight of bolts and arrows.

Unable to force a crossing, Lancaster himself now led his own contingents in an attempt to cross the river at a lower point. Faced by the almost impossibly steep and clay-covered banks of the Ure, they "fought like lions" but were utterly unable to face the resistance of an enemy safely esconced among the reeds on the opposite side of the river, and were forced to give way. At the same time Lord Hereford's troops, led by the Earl in person, attacked the bridge once more. Here the Earl might well have carried the day had it not been that a Welsh soldier, emulating the similar action at Stamford Bridge more than three centuries before, crept below the bridge and thrust a spear through the wooden planking. It so gashed the Earl that he fell dead among his men, who then fled in all directions. Lancaster took refuge in a nearby chapel, and later agreed with Harcla either to surrender or resume battle in the morning. During this period scores of his greatest knights, only too glad to exchange their splendid armour for beggars' rags, crept out into the fields. As daylight approached, Sir Simon Ward, High Sheriff of Yorkshire, called on the Earl to surrender and then led him a prisoner to York. Here a fickle crowd, after pelting the Earl with filth, demanded his immediate execution.

But the King had by now arrived at Lancaster's own castle of Pontefract and demanded that the Earl, together with numerous other distinguished prisoners, be brought before

Opposite: This monument at Alborough originally stood at Boroughbridge, and supposedly commemorates the battle which took place here in 1322 between the Earl of Lancaster and Sir Andrew Harcla.

him. Having spent several weeks incarcerated in "a small square dungeon having only a hole in the roof for entrance," the Earl was put in front of a tribunal of King's men, all determined on his death. The king himself was convinced that Lancaster had been the principal cause of the slaughter of his own favourite, Piers Gaveston. Condemned out of hand, the Earl was forthwith mounted on a wretched nag and plastered with mud and filth, carried to a hill outside the town and there beheaded. "He was," wrote a contemporary, "a man of great wisdom and holy and afterwards did many miracles upon the hill where he was beheaded." Near to this St. Thomas's Hill stood in those days a Cluniac priory in which his body was buried at dead of night. In 1828 a stone coffin was uncovered in Priory Field and thought to be that of the dead earl. It was long preserved at Fryston Hall. Of Lancaster's adherents no less than fourteen knights bachelors and fourteen bannerets were hanged and quartered, although many fled to France and lived to plot the monarch's ruin.

At one time there was erected at Boroughbridge a tall monument to the battle, but this was later removed to Aldborough. As for the old wooden bridge, it was replaced in 1582 and later rebuilt, both in the eighteenth century by Carr of York and later in 1949 by the County Council. In 1792 many bones, pieces of armour and arms were brought to light on the river banks. The church in which Lancaster took shelter was demolished after the battle, but in the present day church there are built into a wall two very ancient representations of the Crucifixion. Taken from the older building they may well have formed part of the altar before which the Earl of Lancaster spent his last night of freedom. The approach to the battlefield in modern times is from beside the bridge and alongside the Navigation Canal.

The Battle of Byland Abbey, 1322.

THE slaughter of Boroughbridge was scarcely over when King Edward II, encouraged by his success against the Earl of Lancaster, determined once more on war with Scotland. Immediately on being warned of the King's intentions, Parliament willingly voted the required funds while every town and village was requested to provide one or more foot soldiers according to wealth or population. Robert Bruce, along with two generals, Murray and Randolph, lost little time in marching an army into England. On August 1st, 1322, Edward advanced against Scotland with forces approximately 100,000 strong, while the Scots—carrying along with them all provender and driving the English sheep and cattle before them to the Border—left the north of England in a state of desolation. Unfortunately Edward had foolishly relied on the country to victual his armies as they marched, and the land before him now lay so bleak and bare that within a few weeks hundreds of his men had died of disease or famine.

The English army was faced not only by Bruce and his generals, but by the spectre of starvation and mutiny. In retreating it vented its wrath by plundering the abbeys of Melrose and Holyrood, and by wounding the monks and stealing the holy pyx from the altar there. At Dryburgh the monastery was completely gutted. Yet so badly had King Edward's plans miscarried that long before he had reached England no less than 20,000 men had been lost by disease and starvation without a blow being struck in battle. Disgraced and scorned, even by the peasants who lined the roads and who claimed that the entire collapse had been brought about by the murder of the Earl of Lancaster, the King finally brought up his army at Blackhowe Moor in the heart of the Yorkshire Hambletons and close beside Byland Abbey. From here an order was sent out to Sir Simon Ward, the High Sheriff, and to Oliver Ingham, Andrew de Harcla, John Darcy, John de Ros, William de Kyme and the Lord Bishop of Durham, demanding their immediate attendance with every man they could command.

Byland Abbey lies in a deep, wild valley, and should have been easily held by any competent army. As for the battlefield itself, few experts have cared to assign the actual site, but it most likely took place at a point called Oldstead Bank, about a mile and a half west of the abbey. The farm buildings here still cover a piece of land known as Scot's Corner.

No sooner had King Edward turned his back on Scotland than an army of Robert Bruce followed closely on his heels. Marching day and night, it burnt Northallerton and other towns as it passed before arriving at Blackhowe Moor. Edward knew nothing of its proximity and, while awaiting the arrival of Harcla with thirty thousand Cumbrians, was spending his time in hunting, feasting and merrymaking. The Scots were prepared to wait for nothing, and having by October 14th discovered the English position, they made a violent attack on its outposts. The Scots fought like madmen to climb the high pathways of the hillside, but time and again the English, commanded by the Earls of Pembroke and Richmond, drove them down the hill. The English archers poured down volley after volley, while spearmen cast down great rocks from high above. Under proper leadership from such a vantage point the English should have been easy victors, but the Scottish commanders realised that their enemies had left their rear entirely unprotected and sent great numbers of forest trained soldiers to circumvent the hill. Thus, even as the English were putting up a tremendous front, these Scottish contingents swept down from above and created such confusion that the English army was reduced to panic.

The result of the battle was disastrous for King Edward. With scores of his greatest leaders killed or taken prisoner, he only escaped "by the very pity of Christ." Always a coward, arrogant and useless in war, he took a swift horse, left his armies to their fate, and did not stop riding until he reached the safety of the coast near Bridlington. In his retreat both the crown jewels and all the royal treasure were left behind. The abbeys of Byland and Rievaulx were raided, the monks being stripped to their skins, and the Scots were soon heard howling their ribaldries along the road to York. According to accepted practice the King lost little time in the apportioning of blame, the scapegoat in this case being Sir Andrew Harcla. Accused of idling around Boroughbridge and of wasting the country instead of hurrying to the King's aid, it was ordered that "Andrew Harcla, late Earl of Carlisle and Warden of the Marches, be first stripped of his knighthood, his golden spurs hacked from his heels, his body to be then hacked into a thousand pieces".

"As for my body," quoth Harcla scornfully, "you may do with it what you will. As for my soul it is a matter for God!" Such was King Edward II of England; a king who but a few years later was himself to meet death at Berkeley Castle, his dying screams of agony and terror ringing out through the black of night.

4: *Bramham and the Roses' Wars*

WHEN King Henry V, hero of Agincourt and great, great grandson of King Edward II, lay breathing his last among the banners of war with France, he may little have thought of the troubles which within a few short years would come to his native land. It was ten years later that the inhabitants of the old Normandy town of Rouen saw Joan of Arc, the Maid of Orleans, put to her death by fire. "God help us!" cried an English soldier "for we have burned a saint!" It must have seemed thirty years later that vengeance had taken its full toll for, following the loss of all her French possessions, the Wars of the Roses split England—and Yorkshire—from end to end. These Wars were in fact very nearly the bane of England. They were fought between 1455 and 1485, but need never have happened if the country had shown a firmer hand in the beginning.

Edward III, son of the weakling, Edward II, had been the father of a number of sons, of whom four only were in succession to the throne. These were Edward the Black Prince, Lionel Duke of Clarence, John of Gaunt and Lancaster, and Edmund Duke of York. The Black Prince died before he could reach the throne and left but a single son, who became King Richard II and was murdered in Pontefract Castle leaving no heir. Next in line should have been Lionel Duke of Clarence, but he died prior to his father and left his claim to his daughter, Phillipa, wife of Edmund, Earl of March. Instead of admitting the claims of Phillipa, Henry (son of the third son, John of Gaunt and Lancaster) usurped the throne and had himself crowned as King Henry IV. He proved to be an excellent king, as did his hero son King Henry V. If only his grandson, King Henry VI, had proved to be anything but a weakling the Lancastrian succession might never have been challenged. But due to the shortcomings of this totally inadequate monarch, the claims of the House of York—and Phillipa—were revived.

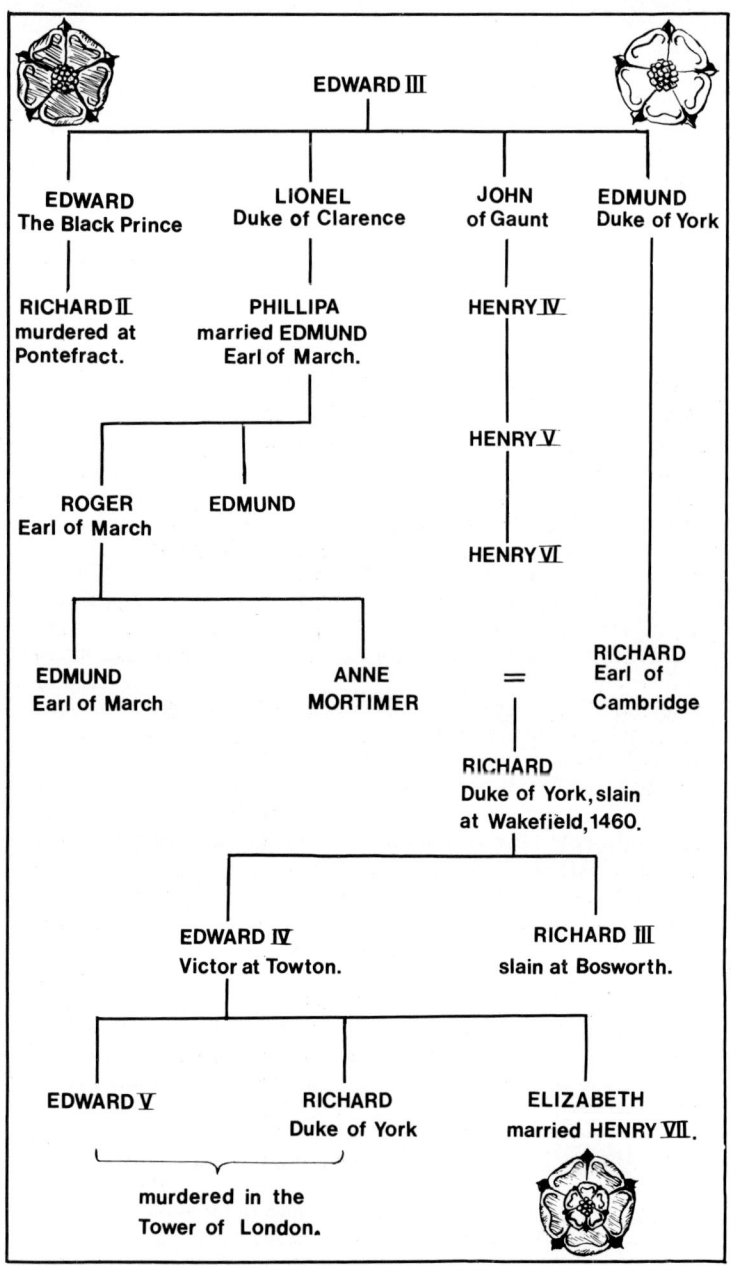

EDWARD III

EDWARD
The Black Prince

LIONEL
Duke of Clarence

JOHN
of Gaunt

EDMUND
Duke of York

RICHARD II
murdered at
Pontefract.

PHILLIPA
married EDMUND
Earl of March.

HENRY IV

ROGER
Earl of March

EDMUND

HENRY V

HENRY VI

EDMUND
Earl of March

ANNE
MORTIMER

=

RICHARD
Earl of
Cambridge

RICHARD
Duke of York, slain
at Wakefield, 1460.

EDWARD IV
Victor at Towton.

RICHARD III
slain at Bosworth.

EDWARD V

RICHARD
Duke of York

ELIZABETH
married HENRY VII.

murdered in the
Tower of London.

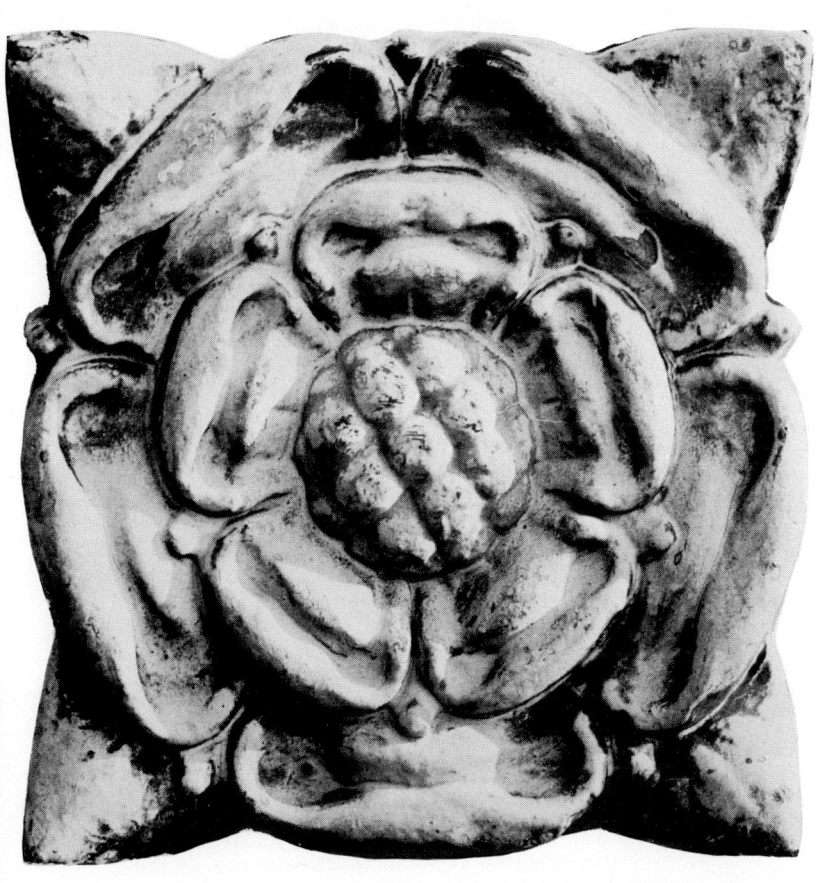

The Roses' Wars. Opposite: Pedigree of the Houses of York and Lancaster.
Above: The Tudor Rose carved in iron on Lendal Bridge, York.

Even King Henry IV—usurper as he was—did not have an easy reign. He was suspected—and in fact accused—of the murder of his cousin, Richard, at Pontefract. Those who yearned after the House of York plotted rebellion against Henry and his House of Lancaster, chief among these plotters being Henry Percy, Earl of Northumberland, who was allied with Thomas Mowbray, Earl Marshall of England. Together with Lords Hastings, Bardolph, Fauconbridge and Sir William Plumpton, they lost little time in attempting to prove the Yorkist point of view. Allied to these lords was Richard Scrope, Archbishop of York and a Yorkshireman to the core, who in preaching in York Minster was sufficiently foolish to state that not only was it the duty of all Englishmen to rise against the King but that Heaven would bless them for so doing. Sent to every church in Yorkshire, the Archbishop's sermon brought hundreds of disgruntled northerners to York. Scrope had at no time intended to do more than harangue the malcontents and return to his home, but unfortunately—as in the case of many such orators—he soon found himself riding at the head of hundreds of rebels to a rendezvous. This was at Shipton, some seven miles north of York.

Ralph Neville, Earl of Westmorland, whose family had almost invariably been opposed to the House of Percy, acted on behalf of the King and, accompanied by Prince John of Lancaster, Lords FitzHugh, Evers and Umfraville, set out to meet the Archbishop and settle the matter for ever. In reply to their query as to why he, a prelate of England, was in arms against his King, the Archbishop replied by handing over a document setting forth the many grievances of the people. Westmorland realised his inability to penetrate the rebel camp and pretended to agree to this document, at the same time suggesting that the Archbishop might well dismiss his followers. The unsuspecting prelate gave the required order, and then both he and Lord Mowbray were promptly arrested and carried to York. At the same time hundreds of rebels returning to their homes were set on by the King's soldiers and either robbed or put to death.

Following their incarceration in York, the Archbishop and Lord Mowbray were hurried to Pontefract Castle where the King awaited them. Here the Archbishop, after pleading in vain for an interview with the king, appealed for his life through his fellow prelate, the Archbishop of Canterbury. In reply to all such pleas the king, anxious only to rid himself of his enemies, replied that "he dared not for the people." The trial of the Archbishop was not long delayed, although Sir

William Gascoigne, a Yorkshireman and Lord Chief Justice of England, refused to conduct it on the grounds that it was illegal. A panel of knights and commoners was then set up on the order of the king. "We adjudge thee, Richard Scrope," said this panel, "as a traitor to the King and do hereby command your immediate execution."

The slaying of the Archbishop was not long delayed. Seated astride a broken horse "of no more than forty pence in value" and mockingly arrayed in a robe of purple, the prelate was led to a cornfield lying between York and Bishopthorpe. Before being beheaded he asked that not one but three wounds be dealt to him in the name of the Five Wounds of Christ. For years following the execution, it was said that the corn grew more richly in this field than in any other around York. So ended the life of Richard Scrope of the great House of Scrope in Wensleydale, and so ended also the lives of all those who dared to raise a sword against the usurper king. Nor was the initial mastery of England by King Henry IV by any means ended by these sacrifices, for the following year came the final settlement of the King's troubles in Yorkshire in the Battle of Bramham Moor.

The Battle of Bramham Moor, 1408.

BRAMHAM Moor lies just to the east of the Great North Road, north of the crossing of the road from Leeds to York and not far south of Wetherby. It is contiguous with many other Yorkshire battlefields including those of Winwoed, Towton and Marston Moor. Here on February 14th, 1408, took place the last battle to be fought in Yorkshire until the coming of the Wars of the Roses.

Immediately following the execution of Scrope, the then Earl of Northumberland and Lord Bardolph, both of whom had been present at Shipton Moor, lost little time in fleeing into Scotland. Scarcely had they arrived than they heard that the Scots intended to betray them to the King of England. They therefore planned another insurrection and with many Scottish soldiers, only too ready for a foray beyond their borders, marched south to Thirsk. Here the rebel lords issued a proclamation informing the people that they had come to comfort the nation, and asked that all who cared for England should come in arms to join them. In their recruiting they experienced very little success, it being remarkable how the English people, enraged in the first place by a usurper king, had grown used to a strong and steady rule. But they persisted

The Battle of Towton, 1461
(see pages 63-69).

in their plans, and the king set forth to make an end of the matter. Sir Thomas Rokeby, High Sheriff of Yorkshire, summoned the soldiers of the county and took control of Knaresborough, being determined to resist the rebels on his own account. On hearing of this move the Earl of Northumberland led his forces to Wetherby and then to Bramham Moor.

Here, within a few hours and flying the banner of St. George, came Sir Thomas Rokeby at the head of the county gentry. Battle was immediately joined, and both sides fought with courage and determination. Very soon, however, the trained soldiers of the Sheriff began to get the better of the rebels, and the Earl's army fled in all directions. Both Northumberland and Bardolph were taken prisoner. Once in York, the trial of the leaders of the rebellion was short and sharp, the Earl being summarily executed and his head being carried in procession before the Sheriff through the city. Following the death of Northumberland, no less than sixteen rebels were hanged and quartered while prosecution of all the insurgents became general throughout the country.

One feels bound to agree with the fairness and justice of the rule of King Henry after the suppression of his more recalcitrant nobles. Had it not been for the almost total inability of Henry VI, England might well have accepted the rule of the House of Lancaster for all time. But to this inability, and despite the courage and resource of Margaret his Queen, then came the Wars of the Roses which were destined to split the nation asunder. The red rose was the emblem of Lancaster and the northern nobles, the white that of the House of York and south. There were fought in swift succession, firstly the Battles of St. Albans, Blore Heath and Northampton, and then the Yorkshire battles of Wakefield and Towton.

The Battle of Wakefield, 1460.

THE Battle of Wakefield was fought on the cold and hard day of December 30th, 1460. In its short but shocking sequences there were slain not only many great nobles, but also Edmund Duke of York, head of his House, and his younger son, the Earl of Rutland.

Queen Margaret, courageous yet vindictive and unscrupulous Queen of the partially imbecile Henry VI of Lancaster, fled into Scotland following the Yorkist victory of Northampton and carried her baby son with her. On receiving news that the Lancastrian lords were assembled in Yorkshire, York had lost little time in marching his armies northwards. From the very first the Duke would appear to have met misfortune or to have been ill–advised. Arriving at Worksop, his advance guard was cut into pieces by a Lancastrian sortie. At the same time he learned that while his own forces numbered but 5,000, those of the Lancastrians totalled four times as many. In no way daunted, however, December 21st beheld this far too optimistic Duke taking up his quarters in his own castle of Sandal near Wakefield. Here, many of the Yorkist army were able to spend Christmas in feasting and merrymaking—the last Christmas that York or his younger son would ever see.

Of Sandal Castle, once the magnificent home of the lords of Wakefield, few traces are extant, although the commanding position remains. Stretching away from the castle an enormous tract of land reaches out into the plains; away to the north it slopes down to the river Calder, while north east lies the town of Wakefield. At the time of the battle the entire district around Sandal would be unenclosed.

Prior to the final meeting of the two armies the Lancastrians had been posted at Pontefract. According to popular belief, provisions in the castle were running low following the Christmas festivities. A foraging party sent out by the Duke of York ventured near the Lancastrian outposts but it was driven home again—surveying the picture today one is apt to wonder what sort of watch was being kept. The main body of the Lancastrian army then advanced on the castle, and managed for the most part to lie in ambush. The Duke, angered by the lack of success of his foragers and with hunger staring his forces in the face, decided to emerge and give battle, apparently being completely unaware of the proximity of the foe. This step was taken in face of the strongest advice to the effect that since reinforcements were hourly expected it would be better to wait.

Emerging from the castle and leading his men in good order, York rode down the hill and charged the enemy with tremendous force. Throughout this very short engagement the Yorkists fought with great gallantry until suddenly the ambuscades which, unknown to the Duke had lain on both sides of the castle, emerged from the scrub. The armed foot under the Earl of Wiltshire and the horse under Lord Rosse then fell on the small Yorkist army with such force that most of its fighters surrendered. The great expanse of Wakefield Green was strewn from end to end with the dead. Among them was the Duke of York, fifty years of age at the time of his death, loved by the common folk and a right and proper king for England.

A. Whisperley '6.

The head of this blameless Duke, sliced off by the orders of Lord Clifford of Skipton, is said to have been carried on the point of a lance as a present to Queen Margaret who was at York. On seeing it she is reputed "firstly to have turned very pale," and then to have given orders that the gory relic should be placed on the ramparts of Micklegate Bar.

The young Duke of Rutland had accompanied his father into the battle, and, in attempting to leave the field, was overtaken by Clifford of Skipton, who demanded his identity. "Spare him," cried the Princes's tutor, Sir Robert Aspsall, "for he is a king's son and good may come to you."

"Whose son is this?" had demanded Clifford, and with the words plunged his dagger into the young man's heart. "By God's blood, thy father slew mine. So will I slay the accursed brood of York!" These were rash words, destined to become the death warrant of Clifford himself a scant few months later at terrible Towton Field.

Leyland, the wandering historian, is said to have visited Wakefield in 1544. He remarked that the place where young Rutland had been killed was "a little above Barres beyond the bridge going up into the town of Wakefield," adding the at that time common belief that the young earl had entered the house of a poor woman when set on by the Lancastrians. She had shut the door and the boy was immediately put to death. The site of this building was formerly claimed to be close to an ancient six-gabled house known as "Six-Chimneys," which was only demolished during the last decade. But it is believed by experts that the slaying took place at the bottom of Kirkgate where it is joined by Park Street. A cross was at one time set up in memory of the sad event. After the battle the severed heads of several prominent Yorkists, including the Earls of Salisbury and Rutland, Sir Richard Limbrick, Sir Edward Bourchier, Sir Thomas Harrington, Sir William Parr, Sir Joseph Pickering, John Harrow, volunteer mercer from London, and John Hanson, probably of the Hansons of Halifax and Huddersfield, were all placed on the walls of York. The head of York himself was surmounted by a paper crown in mockery of his royal aspirations, which were in fact quite

Opposite: The Duke of York fights to the bitter end at the Battle of Wakefield. He was hopelessly outnumbered by the Lancastrians as a result of refusing to await the arrival of reinforcements.

The recently excavated ruins of Sandal Castle, in which the Duke of York took up residence nine days before the Battle of Wakefield. The county town of the West Riding lies in the hollow in the right background.

genuine, and turned city-wards so "that York might overlook the town of York." His body was quietly buried by his friends not far from the church of Pontefract.

It is said that at one time there lay by the road from Wakefield to Sandal a small plot of ground containing a cross which the owners of the land were bound to keep fenced. It was reputedly about four hundred yards distant from the castle, close to the Barnsley road and near to Cock and Bottle Lane, but unfortunately would appear to have been demolished during the Civil Wars. Near to it stood Many Gates Toll Bar, close to which was discovered an old ring engraved with the words "Pour Bon Amour." An ancient willow tree once grew in the vicinity, and it was whispered: "Mind the owd Duke o' York wi'out 'is 'ead as tha goas by th' willer tree!" Wakefield Green has long been almost covered with houses, but bits of bones, broken swords, armour, spurs and other relics have been brought to light from time to time. A monument was erected in 1897.

The Battle of Towton, 1461.

IN March 29th, 1461—Palm Sunday—the Battle of Towton formed an awesome sequel to the Battle of Wakefield. In it are claimed to have perished upwards of 35,000 warriors, mostly of the defeated Lancastrian cause. The combined troops on the field amounted to something over 100,000 men.

After the slaying of the young Earl of Rutland, the hate of the Yorkists for the Lancastrians had known no bounds.

A skirmish had already taken place between the Lancastrian vanguard and the main Yorkist army at Brotherton Marshes beside the river Aire. Retreating from this engagement by way of the little valley of Dintingdale near Saxton, Lord Clifford had met his end when his throat was transfixed by a blunted arrow. In the early morning of Palm Sunday the Yorkist forces marched northwards from Ferrybridge, and lay across the hills just south of Saxton. The Lancastrians, moving up from Tadcaster via the old London road through Stutton and Cocksford, were on the heights above Towton village. Their right wing faced the Yorkist left across what is even today known as Bloody Meadow, while their left wing looked across to the Yorkist Right on the famous field still called North Acres. In case of victory the Lancastrians occupied a splendid position, their only need being to drive the Yorkists southwards along the road they had come and drown them in the river Aire. But in case of defeat their position was frightful. Immediately on their right wing across Bloody Meadow was the deep valley of the Cock Beck, already flooding in the early dawn when they had passed that way and by evening an impenetrable morass. Away to their left beyond the long flats running out towards Cawood and Selby was the equally flooded river Wharfe, swollen by snowstorms and presenting—except beside the bridge of Tadcaster—a position of sheer impossibility.

It was about eleven o'clock in the morning when the Yorkist army moved up from Saxton towards the present day monument, and the battle commenced. From the very first moment of the fight the Lancastrians, commanded by the Earl of Northumberland, Sir Anthony Trollope, Lord Fitz-Hugh and the Earls of Devonshire, Hungerford, Beaumont and Lord Dacres, with the Dukes of Somerset and Exeter commanding the reserves in Towton village, were at a disadvantage. Unable to see their adversaries through a mist of

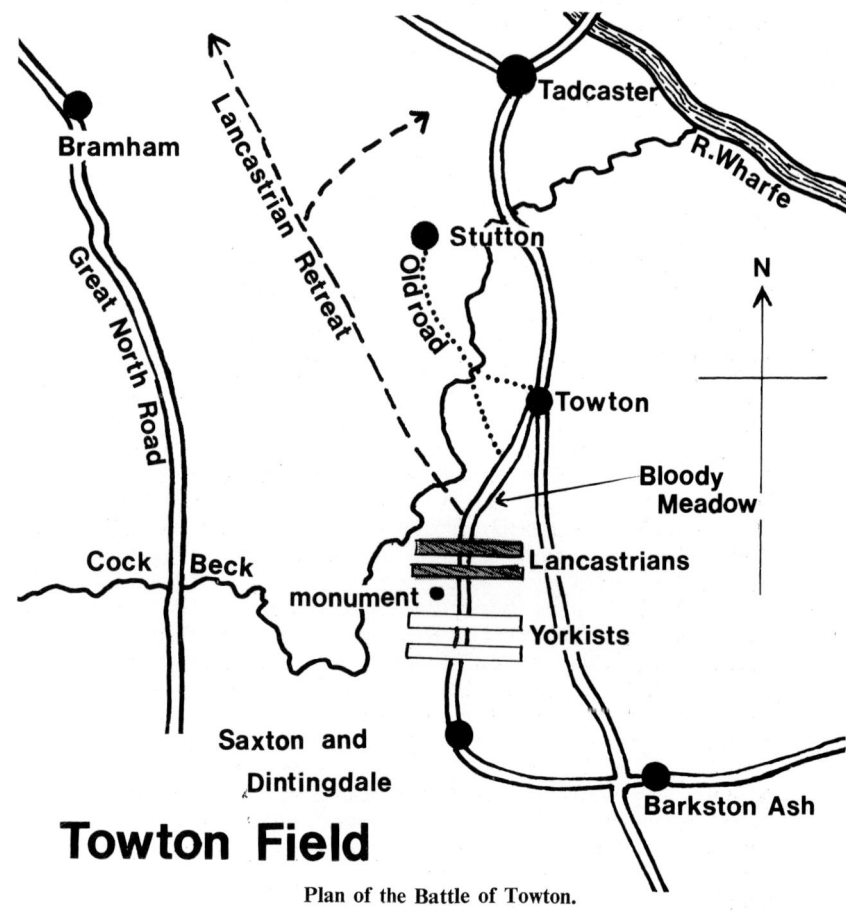

Bramham

Great North Road

Lancastrian Retreat

Tadcaster

R. Wharfe

Stutton

Old road

N

Towton

Bloody Meadow

Cock **Beck**

Lancastrians

monument ●

Yorkists

Saxton and Dintingdale

Barkston Ash

Towton Field

Plan of the Battle of Towton.

snowflakes, their arrows were discharged into the teeth of a storm, only to be returned to the accompaniment of howling laughter from the Yorkist bowmen. These first stepped forward in order to discharge their own flights and the thousands of Lancastrian arrows which had fallen short, and then simply stepped backwards out of range. Realising at last their dreadful predicament, the Lancastrians cast aside their bows and charged southwards. They then closed with the Yorkists in dreadful combat, fighting hand to hand in sleet and bitter cold.

No quarter was asked or given. King Edward, who was on

the field, remembered the deaths of his father and brother at Wakefield and their heads spiked above the gates of York, and saw little cause for mercy. Inch by inch the battle was contested, King Edward leading his forces or assisting the wounded from the fray. Everywhere men were falling fast. Lord Scrope of Bolton was down, while the Lancastrian leader, the Earl of Northumberland, his brother, Sir Richard Percy, Lord Welles and Sir Anthony Trollope all lay face downwards in the snow. Slowly the Lancastrian footmen were driven towards the western edge of the field. Finally, with Yorkist reinforcements under the Earl of Norfolk entering North Acres from Saxton the entire Lancastrian army sped down the hill at the edge of Bloody Meadow. Sliding on the snow-covered hillside, treacherous today as yesterday, thousands of hunted men reached the Cock Beck and splashed through a lake of floodwater towards the plank bridge at Cocksford. With arrows like hail around them, they discovered too late the millstream nature of this spating beck. Fighting took place all round the bridge, which soon gave way, and the stream became packed with drowning men. With horses passing and repassing on this human bridge, the Cock Beck ran red as far as the distant Wharfe.

By four o'clock in the afternoon the cause of the Lancastrian kings was lost for ever. Living warriors lay down to sleep beside the dead. Within a handful of tragic hours on this lonely Yorkshire ridge was altered the story of England. Of the arrests and executions that followed, entire lists are available. King Edward entered York, from where Queen Margaret, her husband, the deposed King Henry and her young son, the so-called Prince of Wales, had fled to Scotland. The heads of the late Duke of York, the Earl of Rutland and Lord Salisbury were taken down to be buried with their bodies, and the usually merciful king, grey with anger at the sight of those gory remains, called for revenge and slaughter. Four executions—the Earl of Devonshire, Sir Baldwin Fulford, Sir William Talboys and Sir William Hill—took place in York, while the Earl of Wiltshire, apprehended at Cockermouth, was beheaded at Newcastle. His head was sent to London to be spiked on London Bridge. Many other prominent Lancastrians were allowed to escape once the King's wrath was cooled, and were later pardoned. A large body of such fugitives sped across the Wharfe at Tadcaster with the Yorkist hunters at their heels, while others took refuge in nearby villages such as Bilbrough.

Most interesting of the stories concerning the dead of

On Towton Field

Above: Cocksford, Towton Dale, scene of the final defeat of the House of Lancaster in the Wars of the Roses. The Lancastrian army poured down the slope in the background to be trapped by the swirling waters of Cock Beck.

Oppostite: Towton Monument broods over Bloody Meadow, a battlefield which on a percentage basis saw an even greater slaughter than the Somme or the Marne.

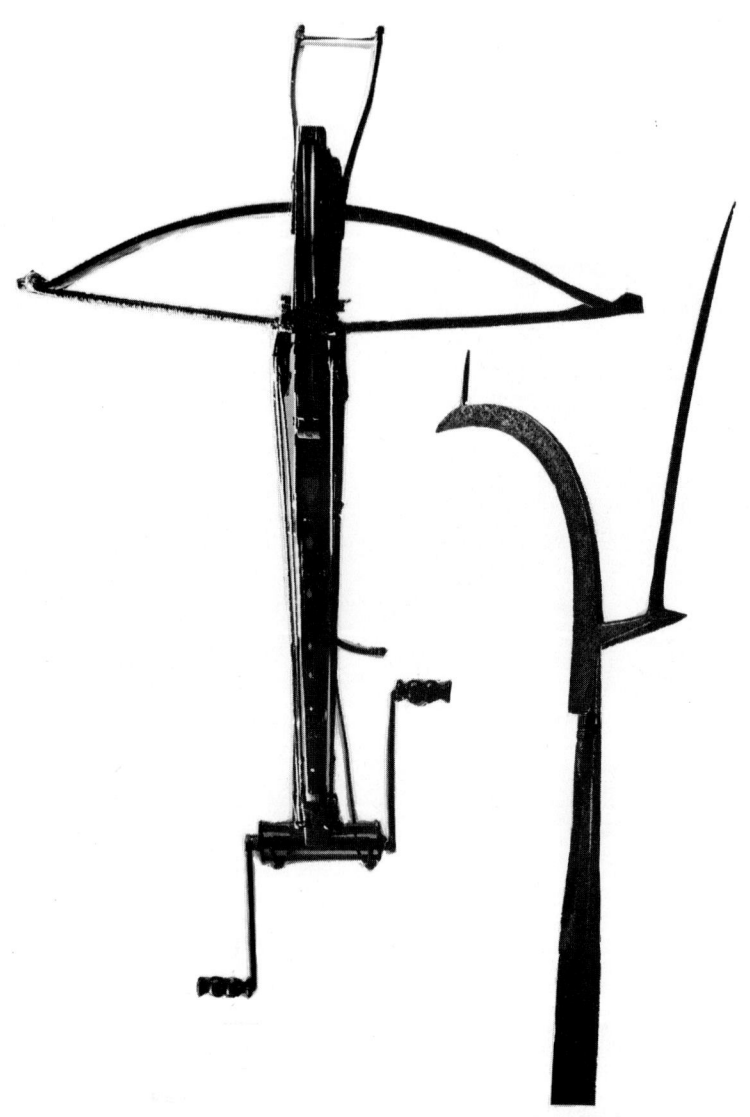

Relics from Towton Field. Left: A crossbow. Right: A gisarm used as a disembowelling knife. (Photos by courtesy of the Castle Museum, York).

Towton is that of Lord Dacres, "slain in the north acres", whose body and that of his war horse lie buried in Saxton churchyard. The skull of the charger was excavated in 1861. It was at Saxton also that hundreds of warriors, including Lord Clifford were buried in an enormous grave. Until a few years ago there still lay among the furrows of Bloody Meadows, as well as beside the beck below, the graves of hundreds more. Saddest of the legends on this dreadful field is that of the discovery of an ancient ring, turned up by some whistling ploughman. On this ring, gift of some maid to a knight of Towton long ago, was inscribed "En loial amour tout de mon coer." Another such ring, preserved today by the Dukes of Northumberland, bears the words, "Now is thys", together with the Percy Lion. To balance such stories is the tale of the wild, white Yorkist rose, still stained with the blood of Lancaster, pigment from bones, blood and armour in that dreadful soil. Even today one may well call up the ghosts of Towton Field by walking the old road which branches away from the inn at Towton. and passes over the hill to meander through scrub and gorse to the still-existent Cocksford on the track to Stutton. Such indeed was Towton with a list of dead such as no battle in Europe—even the Somme or the Marne—may compare on a percentage basis.

5: *The Tudor Rebellions*

WITH the end of the Roses' Wars and with King Henry VII on the throne of England, the country remained at peace until the days of Henry VIII and the Tudor rebellions. Many historians have written of Henry VIII—his ambitions, his casting out of foreign influences and his setting up as head of the English Church. For centuries English kings had been at loggerheads with the popes, although the mysteries of the "older faith" had been part and parcel of England. In Yorkshire the people had come to revere the monastic system in which abbeys such as Fountains, Rievaulx, Byland, Jervaulx, Bolton and Kirkstall had played so great a part. When these were threatened by the so-called Dissolution, hundreds of northern people began to condemn the king. It is true that the monks with their ever-increasing institutions had become something of a handicap to advancement. But at the same time little assistance was being given to the north of England and much was being suppressed, especially by adventuring merchants from the south who snatched the abbey lands as soon as they fell vacant and cared little for the poorer northern folk. The position was in no way alleviated by the sudden news that Yorkshire and Lincolnshire must be prepared to face the closing down of no less than forty of the smaller religious houses. Hence arose the Pilgrimage of Grace.

The Pilgrimage of Grace, 1536.

THIS rebellion began in Lincolnshire in the little town of Louth. Within weeks its adherents were demanding that the king should close no more abbeys or monasteries and that he should rid himself of his minister, Thomas Cromwell. As head of the Church it was expected that Henry would accede to these demands, but by this time the position had become out of hand with 40,000 rebels having entered Lincoln. At the same time there arrived a messenger from Yorkshire stating that thousands were in arms and ready to march, only being held in check by a fear of mob violence. Within a few weeks the north discovered a leader in Robert Aske, who came from Aughton where his family had resided for centuries. Aske was a man of mild views, and on being appointed captain of the so-called "Pilgrims" he issued articles emphasising the religious angle and forbidding pillage. He soon had the entire county of Yorkshire at his side. Thousands of Yorkshiremen assembled at Market Weighton, and marched towards Ponte-fract where they were joined by Lord Darcy, Governor of the Castle, and the Archbishop of York. From first to last it was laid down that no violence was intended, and that the only wish of the malcontents was to meet the king. But the fact that Aske was keeping up the state of a prince infuriated Henry, who also became indignant that the Pilgrimage should have reached such proportions. He sent up his envoys with instructions to pretend to treat with the rebels at Doncaster. Aske was taken in by this move, and removed his badges before foolishly instructing his rebels to disperse. He was very soon arrested. Having gained control, the king ordered the arrest of all similar leaders, and wasted no time in putting them to death. Chief among these were Aske himself who was hanged at York, Lord Darcy and Sir Robert Constable who were beheaded in London, the Lady Bulmer who was burned at the stake—the common penalty for women caught in treason—and Nicholas Tempest of Bracewell and the Abbots of Fountains and Jervaulx who were quartered at Tyburn. Of Adam Sedbar, Abbot of Jervaulx, it is told how he was unwilling to join the rebels and was threatened by the captains with the burning of his abbey. Fleeing to the woods and seeing smoke rising from the building he returned to them and thus signed his death warrant. The vengeance of the King was in fact mild in comparison with the penalties for rebellion in other parts of Europe.

The Rebellion of the Northern Earls, 1569.

PERHAPS the most devastating insurrection ever to take place in Yorkshire was the Rebellion of the Northern Earls in 1569. In view of the difficulties of his day and age, the action of Henry VIII in closing down the monasteries and his reprisals against the rebels of the "Pilgrimage of Grace," had shown a certain competent statesmanship. With the death

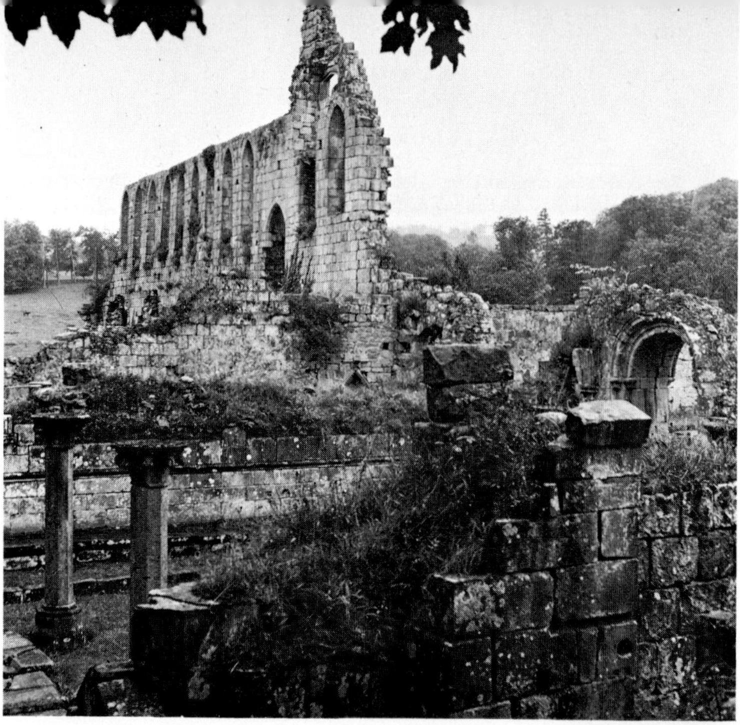

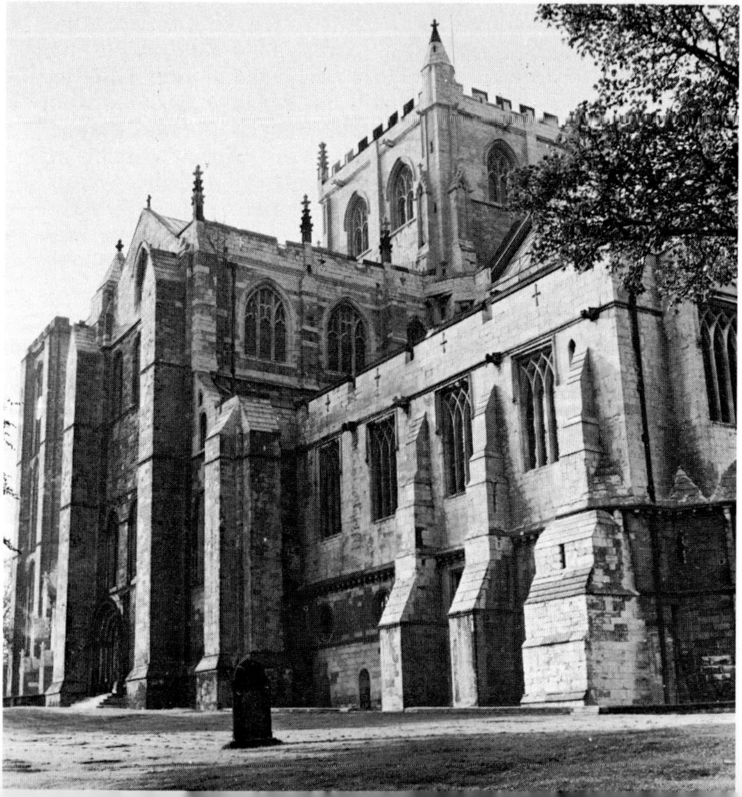

Scenes of Tudor Rebellion

Above: The moated Markenfield Hall, home of Sir Thomas Markenfield who fled to France after being involved in the Rebellion of the Northern Earls.

Opposite page, top: Jervaulx Abbey, a principal scene of the Pilgrimage of Grace in 1536. Adam Sedbar, Abbot of Jervaulx, joined the Pilgrimage only because the rebels threatened to set fire to the abbey.

Opposite page, bottom: Ripon Cathedral, where participants in the Rebellion of the Northern Earls took the sacrament before marching south.

of Henry, followed soon afterwards by that of his young son, Edward VI, the accession of Queen Mary brought an attempt to restore England to her "older faith." Unfortunately Mary chose the wrong means to an end, and there was considerable strife. With the coming of Elizabeth, there was a certain amount of religious toleration, but always accompanied by a plain warning that death would be the penalty for plotting against the throne. This was the position in 1569 when the Earls of Westmorland and Northumberland sought to arrange a marriage between the Queen of Scots, as representative of the Catholic Party, and the Duke of Norfolk. The Duke was promptly arrested, and the Earls then placed themselves at the head of numerous Catholic families which had suffered bitterly under the Dissolution of the Monasteries. The Yorkshire leaders of the proposed rebellion included old Richard Norton, a religious enthusiast, of Rilston Castle near Skipton and of Norton Conyers near Ripon. Another was Sir Thomas Markenfield of Markenfield Hall, Ripon, a young aristocrat, self-exiled on account of his faith and spoiling for trouble, having spent much of his time as a student of theology in Rome.

It was late autumn of 1569 when the drums of rebellion were beaten in the north, and the Earls first met at Northumberland's house at Topcliffe, near Thirsk. Here the rebels informed Northumberland, who had suddenly evinced little heart for the project, that should he at this juncture fail to throw in his lot they would vent their rage on him. At the same moment there came to the ears of all concerned the sound of the Topcliffe church bells being rung backwards, a sign that the rebellion was launched. There also came news that Wilstrop, one of the queen's captains, was on his way to arrest them all. This was totally false, but the rebel leaders retired to Brancepeth Castle on the Durham border, carrying with them the unwilling Earl. Lord Sussex, the queen's General, received orders to warn all justices and constables to keep watch and ward, and placed the towns of Hull, Pontefract and Knaresborough in a state of defence. On October 14th he reported to the queen that all was safe, giving the names of the Yorkshire leaders as Norton, Markenfield, Hussey and Danby— every one a friend of the Queen of Scots in whose favour the rebellion had been intended.

By November 2nd Sussex had commanded the Earls of Northumberland and Westmorland to appear at York in order to answer for their conduct. On being informed that they had gone to Brancepeth, he ordered a general mobilisation of the county and called on the nobility and gentry to support him.

Two days later he became even more insistent when told that the rebels had entered Durham Cathedral, celebrated Mass and torn up the prayer book. But little notice was taken of Sussex's demands, "as few as possible riding in and far more going to join the rebels." At this juncture it was becoming obvious to him that this part of the country either could not or would not defend itself.

At Brancepeth the Earls were beginning to lose heart, and under these circumstances were making it plain that their enmity was not against the queen but her advisers. Several of the plotters—despite growing support—were joining Northumberland in saying that, with the arrest of the Duke of Norfolk, the rebellion should be ended. But Lady Westmorland, sister of Norfolk, insisted on it being continued. The rebels then immediately moved southwards via Darlington, Richmond and Thirsk to Ripon, where they fell in with Norton and Markenfield carrying the banner of the "Five Wounds of Christ" and the motto "God us Ayde." In pitiful support of these grandiloquent effects there was also flaunted "Speed the Plough," the motto of the starving farmers who were suffering from the snatching of the abbey lands. Throughout a bitter December day, hundreds of rebels stood shivering in Ripon market place, while drums were beaten and speeches flung against the sky. Soon, to the deep boom of the Minster bells, men clad in white armour went marching or riding into the empty nave of the great church, and partook the sacrament. Finally, marching out of Ripon, the late sunshine catching the glint of mail and the shimmering of the Norton banners, the entire rebel army went tramping south.

In London the queen was moving her pieces on the board. Her orders were rampant: "Advise Lord Essex to step up his action against the rebels. Advise Sir George Bowes to hold Barnard Castle. Call upon Sir Ralph Sadler. Close me the Scottish borders and the coast, with these all chance of assistance or escape for these rebels." As the line of the insurgent armies stretched slowly from Richmond and Ripon towards Wetherby, Knaresborough, Tadcaster and Cawood, there came news that the queen's generals in the north were moving in for the kill. What happened next is dubious, but the rebellion which had arisen like a moor fire died in just the same way. If the insurgents had kept going towards London how different might have been their story, but abysmal leadership meant that the rebellion was now over.

Much has been told of the flight of the Earls for the heather; the fleeing of old Norton and young Markenfield into France;

and of the men of Ripon who esconced themselves on their own doorsteps to await the queen's wrath. Several of the sons of Richard Norton were lodged in the Tower of London, and had been hanged by April. Sir Fletcher Norton, the first Lord Grantley, became the eventual sole representative of this once-celebrated Yorkshire family. Wordsworth tells the story of the family in his *White Doe of Rilston,* mentioning Emily Norton who, accompanied by a tame white doe given by one of her brothers, trod the mountain turf between Rilston Castle and Bolton Priory. There she knelt in prayer for her lost menfolk, the distant bells of Rilston playing "God us Ayde." But there was a more tempestuous side of the rebellion —the examples needed to be made; the threats against England by foreign powers ready at all times to use her so-called rebels as a shield; the gallows erected throughout the north; and the entire, tragic story of bitter religious and political controversy, broken monasteries and broken promises.

There are no set situations from which one may review the rebellion. Ripon market place stands much as it ever stood, as do Ripon Minster, Brancepeth Castle and Durham Cathedral. Rilston Castle is no more than a few deep tracings among the grass, but Norton Conyers, once a home of the Nortons but now of the Grahams, is still a glorious old house. Markenfield Hall, one of the old manor houses of Yorkshire, is open to the public on certain summer days.

6: *The Civil Wars*

FEW chapters of history can appeal more strongly than those of the Civil Wars, the reason being that these battles lie nearer to our own times. When Charles I unfurled his standard against his own people at Nottingham in 1642, there commenced a struggle which not only ended regal autocracy in Britain but gave to the nation the priceless gift of constitutional government. During centuries, English kings had been virtual dictators. Nevertheless, slowly but surely the character of the people had been emerging. With the Roses' Wars and the slaughtering in battle of hundreds of warmongering barons, the rights of the ordinary man were becoming a potent force. By the time of Elizabeth, the queen was openly stating that without the assistance of the people there was nothing, but with them everything.

It was into this picture of growing freedom that in 1603 there stepped King James I of England and VI of Scotland. Steeped in theories concerning the divine rights of kings, James thrust these beliefs on his family. Charles I was thus trained from boyhood in such ways of thinking and, encouraged by well-meaning advisers like Strafford and Laud, set out to become a king indeed. From the first, Parliament was not disposed to accept his convictions. Time after time the king laid down his tenets concerning the blank obedience due from the subject, but Parliament repeatedly emphasised not only its right to represent the people but to question any who might become dangerous to the State. Thus time after time the parliament of the moment found itself dissolved and sat back to watch the king and his Council imprison many of the wisest men in England.

Oddly enough the first people to show a national resentment to Charles's arbitrary methods were his late father's own countrymen, the Scots, who were soon to invade the English border. It was following the partial settlement of these Scottish hostilities that Yorkshire, sickened of armies living off the county and injuring local trade, made few bones of the fact that she had no wish for war. The troubles between king and people, however, were fast deepening and men were taking sides. Here and there among Yorkshire's ruling classes, mostly Royalist, were emerging individuals who, despite centuries of family loyalty to the throne, had developed feelings of affection towards the common folk. They were also indignant about the punishments meted out by the king's advisers towards patriots such as John Hampden, Lilburne and Prynne. Among these the greatest were the Fairfaxes. Sprung from a line of statesmen, thinkers and soldiers, and unbiassed in any political direction, they were simple churchmen and upholders of the law. Sir Thomas Fairfax — "Black Tom" to the people—was respected by all Yorkshiremen, especially those among the woollen textile areas where many had been ruined by recent military occupation.

It was Thomas Fairfax who finally bearded the king when he arrived in the north intent on levying Yorkshire troops. Charles called a meeting of the county on Heworth Moor, near York. Accompanied by a glittering throng of adherents and watched by some 60,000 Yorkshiremen, he spoke kindly to the crowd and exhorted their help in maintaining religion, liberty, law and peace, few of which had in fact been very royally maintained during the last few years. With such words the king would have dismissed the crowd, but certain gentry of the county had drawn up a petition setting forth the miseries being suffered by many families and beseeching the king to think again. Such a petition, coming from responsible gentry, farmers and freeholders, should at least have been received with courtesy. Instead it was snatched and trampled, until finally Sir Thomas Fairfax dismounted from his horse and succeeded in thrusting the petition beneath the royal saddle bow. What happened next was witnessed by thousands. The king, a magnificent equestrian, caused his charger to rear and almost rode Fairfax to the ground. Ill-advised as ever and backed by scores of scoffing cavaliers, Charles according to his wont had done the wrong thing. "Black Tom," swinging away from Heworth towards his home at Nun Appleton, came to the conclusion that although his loyalty to the throne might have been strong, this particular king had little claim to his future allegiance except under the control of Parliament. It was during the following August that Charles, acting on his own initiative in raising his standard at Nottingham, made plain his intentions of fighting a civil war. which in due course came to Yorkshire.

The Battles of the West Riding.

THE Fairfaxes, with many other gentlemen of the West Riding took sides with Parliament. At first Lord Fairfax had attempted neutrality, but any such plan proved to be hopeless. On September 27th, 1642, the old lord accepted the post of Commander-in-Chief for the Parliament in Yorkshire, with his son, Sir Thomas, as Commander-of-Horse. By December, however, Lord Fairfax was informing Parliament that he was already in the greatest straits for supplies. On the Royalist side, the queen was pawning her jewels in Holland in order to raise more funds for the king. Charles, accompanied by a slender band of followers, had moved west from Nottingham to recruit troops on the Welsh borders where Lord Essex, the Parliamentary General, seemed unwilling to chance his hand. From this point the king, after making an initial attempt on London only to be frustrated by the Battle of Edgehill, was joined at Oxford by his brilliant yet impetuous nephew, Prince Rupert. It now became plain that the royal objective from first to last must be London. The Royalist General Hopton was ordered to bring up troops from Devon and Cornwall, and Lord Newcastle was to move southwards out of Yorkshire while the king brought an army out of Wales.

Lacking coherent plans, the Parliamentarians soon found themselves on the defensive. Nevertheless, an army under the Parliamentary General Waller was sent to check Hopton in the west while Oliver Cromwell held the east country and the Fairfaxes the north. In this reign the Royalist headquarters were at York, and a strong garrison was at Pontefract Castle. At the outset of the war Lord Newcastle had considered there would be no difficulty in securing Yorkshire but Lord Fairfax, lying at Tadcaster, had been able to check his advance. Parliament also held the seaports of both Hull and Selby, while hundreds of ill-armed yet enthusiastic amateur soldiers of the West Riding were preparing for battle. It was in November that the first skirmish was fought in Yorkshire at Wetherby when Sir Thomas Fairfax, accompanied by some 300 foot and 40 horse, was attacked by about twice that number of Royalists creeping out of some woods. At the moment of the alarm Fairfax had been preparing to ride to Tadcaster; he seized a horse and accompanied by only four of his pikemen at first held the enemy alone. "Everybody had a shot at him," later wrote an eye-witness, "he holding them with his sword, then backing amongst his pikes." After the rest of Fairfax's

Tadcaster bridge, setting for a skirmish in the Civil Wars. Lord Fairfax's main Parliamentary forces were outnumbered by 3,000 men, but managed to hold the bridge from morning until afternoon. Troops also came this way after the Battle of Towton.

small "army" had turned out, a short struggle took place during which Fairfax's powder magazine was blown up. The Royalists, believing this was the opening of cannon fire, fled back to York with Fairfax's horsemen at their heels.

By December, Sir Thomas was back in Tadcaster where Lord Fairfax's main Parliamentary forces were drawn up in order to meet an advance which the Royalists were making towards the manufacturing towns of the West Riding. Outnumbered by 3,000 men, father and son still managed to hold Tadcaster bridge from morning until afternoon but only with heavy loss. Captain Lister, an invaluable officer, was slain and all the ball and powder spent. On this catastrophe the Parliamentary forces fell back to Cawood. Sir Thomas met a large Royalist contingent in a narrow lane at Sherburn-in-Elmet, but broke through its baricades. Even though his horse was shot under him, he managed to escape to Selby.

The Royalist Lord Newcastle, having in the meantime taken the town of Leeds, made a swift attack on Bradford. Here the Parliamentary resistance was tremendous. The townsmen, armed mainly with such weapons as scythes, were virtually leaderless but were determined to give up only with their lives. Heavy fighting broke out all around present day Forster Square, and the Royalists set up their cannon at Undercliffe and Barkerend in order to bombard the church. Time after time the forty odd musketeers of the town, lurking among the houses, drove out the Royalists. Then Captain Hodgson, a trained soldier from Halifax, arrived to take over the Parliamentary command. Among the narrow streets the guns of Sir William Savile, the Royalist commander, were virtually useless, while the greater the confusion the better the townsmen fought. The struggle continued until the arrival of Sir Thomas Fairfax who, having resolved to attack Leeds, sallied forth from Bradford at the head of some 3,000 musketeers and local volunteers or "clubmen."

Hearing of this march, Sir William Savile entrenched himself at the head of a small army in central Leeds. In those days the main street of this town was already known as Briggate and —as today—ran down to a bridge over the river Aire. In his attack on Leeds, Fairfax divided his forces. Some 1,000 men left Bradford for Hunslet to attack Briggate from the bridge, while the rest approached the town via Apperley Bridge, Cookridge and Woodhouse Moor. On reaching a spot now close to Leeds University, a trumpeter was dispatched to suggest surrender. The Royalists refused. Deep entrenchments were made by Sir William Savile; these ran all the way from Upperhead towards the river with breastworks at Boar Lane junction and more entrenchments guarding the bridge. Savile trained his guns along Briggate, and at four o'clock in the afternoon Fairfax opened his attack. Charging the earthworks to an accompaniment of mighty cheering and a great deal of hand-to-hand fighting, he fought his way towards the bridge. Simultaneously his Hunslet contingents arrived on the south side of this structure. Sergeant Major Forbes, a Parliamentary officer, drove many Royalists down towards the bridge where a number were drowned. He then heard renewed cheering from the Boar Lane and Briggate junction which told him the town was taken. With prisoners everywhere and heavy gains in powder and shot, Sir Thomas now lost little time in driving his fleeing foes to Wakefield where a capitulation took place.

The Royalist Earl of Newcastle retreated to York and sat

down to await the arrival of the queen. She landed at Bridlington, bringing new hope as well as a great deal of money to the Royalist cause. The position in Yorkshire for the Parliamentarians now rapidly deteriorated, most of the gentlemen of the East Riding having little use for battles fought in the commercial west. Among the defecting gentry was Sir Hugh Cholmeley who had given up Scarborough to the king. The Hothams, following their original refusal to allow the king to enter Hull, were now veering towards the Royal cause—a decision for which they were later to pay with their lives.

Lord Fairfax now determined to fall back out of Selby to Leeds, and Sir Thomas was ordered to act as decoy. While the old lord and some 2,000 troops made their way across a hostile country, Sir Thomas advanced towards Tadcaster, his plan being to lure the Royalists to this town and then to get away via Bramham Moor. This would draw the Royalist General Goring further and further from the main Parliamentary forces. Unfortunately the orders of Lord Fairfax partially miscarried when Sir Thomas and his small company were attacked on Seacroft Moor and utterly defeated. At Kiddal Hall, which lies in the hollow of the road from Seacroft to York, one of the Royalist Ellis family reputedly refused assistance to some Parliamentary soldiers and was slain by them. His ghost was said to haunt the precincts of this fine old house.

Sir Thomas Fairfax, now master of both Leeds and Bradford, soon decided on the subjection of Wakefield which was occupied by about 1,000 Royalist horse and foot. Having only two main streets branching away from the Market Place, the town had been easily fortified with all alleys barricaded and cannon in the streets. On his arrival, Fairfax ordered one body of his troops to attack the hedges north of the town while the other attempted the Norgate barricades. For over two hours the fighting was desperate, until the Parliamentarians secured one of the cannon, turned it on the defenders, and thus forced the barricades. Fairfax himself now led a troop of cavalry through the streets, routed the Royalists, and took Lord Goring prisoner. He rode away accompanied by his lordship towards what he thought were his own contingents, but found himself among the enemy. Fairfax only escaped by leaping his horse across a hedge, while, to his eternal credit, Goring did nothing to stop him. News was later carried to the Parliamentary leaders that not only had Wakefield fallen but no less than 1,500 prisoners and many stands of ammunition had been taken. From end to end of England, Fairfax's brilliant exploit was the talk of fighting men. But brilliant as such exploits may have been, the victory was fruitless for neither Lord Fairfax nor Sir Thomas were able to hold on to their gains. Nor did the luck of the Parliamentary armies turn, despite the acquisition of some 2,000 "valiant men of Manchester, most of whom turned out to be arrant cowards. The Battle of Adwalton Moor almost ended the Parliamentary cause for ever.

The Battle of Adwalton Moor, 1643.

ADWALTON Moor lies three miles south-west of Bradford and midway along the present day Leeds and Whitehall Road at Drighlington. It was on June 30th, 1643, that the Fairfaxes heard Lord Newcastle was on his way to Bradford and, having only ten days' provisions, decided they had best forestall the Royalist arrival by falling on their army at Adwalton. Unfortunately the Royalists had become aware of this plan, and had placed in the field their entire army of 7,000 horse and 11,000 foot against Fairfax's surprise party of a mere 3,000. Sir Thomas himself was in command of the Parliamentary Right Wing of 1,000 foot and five troops of horse, and not only withstood the charges of the Royalist cavalry but successfully resisted the foot. Despite the overwhelming odds, the Parliamentary chances seemed fair until their heady success caused them to engage the enemy too far. The Royalists then sent numerous troops of horse and foot by a still-existing lane to fall on the Parliamentary rear. Fairfax only saved his army by the loss of five hundred men and by retreating down a by-lane which, passing not far from Oakwell Hall, carried him via Birstall and Cleckheaton to Bailiff Bridge and Halifax. Only 200 of Manchester's levies were intact, the rest having returned into Lancashire.

The defeat of their army at Adwalton was a bitter blow for the Parliament. The Royalists on the other hand were jubilant, the queen writing to Lord Newcastle in York begging him to clear the county. At the same time her own intrigues with the Hothams had almost succeeded in placing Hull in Royalist hands. Sir Thomas Fairfax forced his way to Leeds, and met with even greater misfortune when, following his main army towards Hull and passing through Selby, he was attacked by Royalist cavalry, wounded and only through sheer genius managed to get his troops beyond the town. He spent no less than 22 hours on horseback without either food or drink, his small daughter fainting on his saddle bow. Never had the

Lone rider on Adwalton Moor, scene of the defeat of Lord Fairfax following the Siege of Bradford. The Parliamentary surprise party of 3,000 men was outnumbered by 18,000 Royalists.

Parliamentary cause seemed so grim, for victory after victory was coming to the Royalists elsewhere. In the west country, Hopton, the King's General, was doing all in his power to join up with the king, capturing both Bristol and Taunton and covering himself with glory at Roundaway Down.

The Parliamentary cause was only being saved by the fact that Plymouth and Hull were still in their hands, and by the almost incredible foolishness of Lord Newcastle in suddenly turning away from Yorkshire in order to attack Cromwell's so-called Eastern Association in East Anglia. Quarreling with his subordinates, it was only this Royalist altercation which gave the Fairfaxes a chance of respite. In the final decision of Newcastle to return to Hull, it also brought Cromwell and his famous "Ironsides" across the Humber. From the moment of their meeting Cromwell and Fairfax formed a strong friendship. Each had had his victories and each his defeats, but now they together began to turn the war. It had been at Winceby in Lincolnshire that they had first charged the enemy in unison, and few greater stories of dash and courage can be told in the annals of war. Lord Manchester had written that "Colonel Cromwell charged with my regiment and his own with the greatest honour, whilst Sir Thomas Fairfax who is a person that exceeds any expression as a commander of valor, performed his duty with success." With Lord Newcastle lying first before Hull and then retreating to York, the war passed for a time out of Yorkshire to return in 1644 when the cause of King Charles was ended for ever on the field of Marston Moor.

Marston Moor, 1644.

MARSTON Moor was fought on the evening of July 2nd 1644. It was the last great battle of the Civil Wars except for Naseby and one of the last to be fought on English soil. For some time the Royalist forces under the Marquis of Newcastle and Sir Thomas Glemham had been couped in York. The Parliamentary army was unable to encircle the walls, since any such movement would have entailed finding extra troops. It was short of food and water, as were the Royalists within the city, and lay encamped among the fields. Under such circumstances, the Parliamentary Generals, Lord Fairfax, the Scottish Earl of Leven, Sir David Leslie, Oliver Cromwell and Sir Thomas Fairfax, sensed a dangerous stalemate, and wrote a letter to the Earl of Manchester imploring his aid. Manchester soon arrived at the head of a large army and the city was blockaded. On Friday, June 25th, however, there was brought to the Parliamentary generals the news that Prince Rupert, Commander in Chief of the Royal armies, had heard of Newcastle's plight in York and was advancing at the head of 10,000 horse and 8,000 foot. He intended to relieve the city and give battle to the Parliament.

The Parliamentary staff agreed they would wait two days to see whether reinforcements might reach them from the Midlands. On being informed that these auxiliaries could not get to Wakefield before July 4th, it was then resolved that York be abandoned. The Parliamentary forces were withdrawn from the city to Marston Moor to await the arrival of the Prince, but Rupert had no intention of passing through the hostile lower West Riding. He played a different card, marching out of Lancashire via Clitheroe, Skipton and

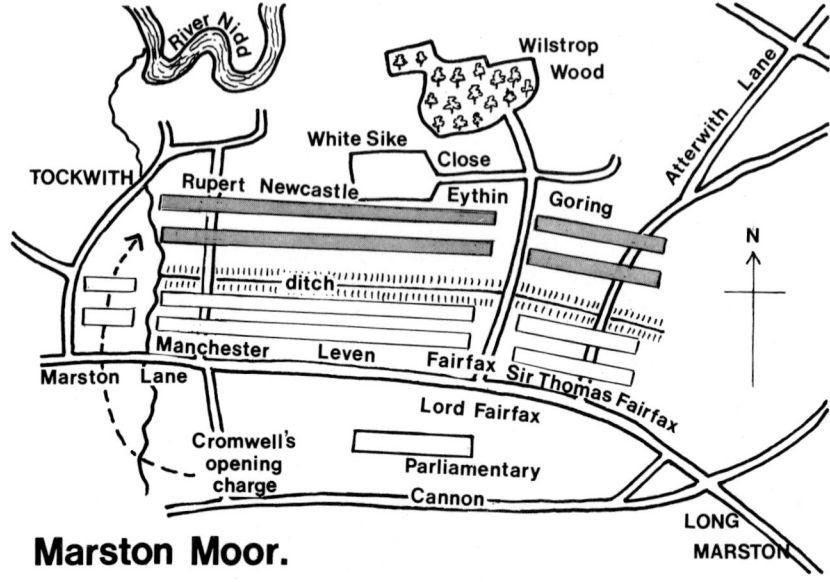

Marston Moor.

Plan of the Battle of Marston Moor.

Knaresborough to Boroughbridge. He then sent out a flying squadron of horse to intimidate the Parliamentarians north of the Moor at Skip Bridge, and crossed the Swale at Thornton Bridge to approach York via Tollerton and the east bank of the Ouse. Leaving his main forces encamped some five miles north of the city, Rupert is said to have entered York in time to meet Lord Newcastle who detested the "German princeling." The Marquis lost little time in proclaiming that in his own opinion and that of his lieutenant, Lord Eythin, no battle should be fought. In reply Rupert is said to have retorted angrily that he had in his possession a letter from the king ordering him to fight—a letter which was never seen in his lifetime but when discovered after his death was found to have advised him to fight "if necessary."

On Marston Moor the Parliamentarians also believed there would be no battle. Hoping to bar the road along which Rupert might march south to meet the king, they prepared to evacuate the field. The early morning of July 2nd beheld the entire

Parliamentary army in retreat towards Tadcaster. The Scottish regiments leading the van were hungry and without water, and had almost reached their destination when Sir Thomas Fairfax, bringing up the rear with Cromwell and Leslie, was astounded to see the scarlet and gold of Royalist cavalry entering the Moor. Realising the danger of a rearguard action, Fairfax lost little time in sending his trumpeters to recall the troops to the field. By two o'clock in the afternoon two great armies comprising in all some 50,000 troops, almost equally divided, lay facing each other across the scrub.

Marston Moor lies seven miles west of York and is bounded on the east by Atterwith Lane (now Station Lane) and Long Marston, on the south by Bilton, on the west by Tockwith and on the north-east by Skip Bridge and Wilstrop Wood. Between Long Marston and Tockwith is Marston Lane, near which lay the Parliamentary army while that of the Royalists was across the Moor. Standing today beside the tall and grey monument in Marston Lane, it is easy to plan the fight. Immediately behind the watcher as he gazes along the grassy track known as Moor Lane, rises the shallow height of Marston Hill on which the Parliament had set its cannon. Four hundred yards along Moor Lane to the left of the track is a small pond, to the right and left of which there ran at the time of the battle a deep ditch. It has long been filled in, but was then lined with dense scrub and stretched from Marston to Tockwith, a distance of one and a half miles. Further along Moor Lane the track comes to four lane ends, of which the right runs into the fields, the central towards Wilstrop Wood where much fighting took place, and the left in a wide grassy "ride" towards White Syke Close. Here, towards the end of the battle were slain a thousand of Newcastle's famous "Whitecoats."

Ashe, who was Cromwell's chaplain, wrote: "How goodly a sight was this, to behold two mighty armies which with flying colours did look each other in the face."

"You cannot imagine," commented another eye witness, "the courage, spirit and resolution that was taken up on both sides for we looked and they also upon this fight as losing or gaining the garland."

Throughout the afternoon neither side seemed willing to commence action, perhaps because of the ditch and thorn. Along Marston Lane, all the way from Tockwith village to the foot of the present-day monument, were thousands of Parliamentary troops. At distant Tockwith was the Parliamentary left wing, comprising eight troops of dragoons under Colonel

Frizeal supported by three regiments of Scottish horse under Sir David Leslie and 38 troops of Lord Manchester's horse with the famous "Ironsides" under Cromwell. Further along the lane towards the monument were some 3,000 of Manchester's foot under the Scottish General Crawford.

Facing this Parliamentary left wing near Tockwith but further out on the moor were the Royalist right wing—5,000 horse under Prince Rupert. Stretching away from the Prince across the moor lay some 7,000 troops under Lords Byron, Grandison and the Royalist Colonels Russell, Porter, Bellasis and O'Neil. Beside White Syke Close were the famous "Whitecoats" under Lord Eythin. The whole of this Royalist centre was facing that of the Parliament which comprised some 9,000 of the Earl of Cassilis's Scottish foot brigaded with the Fifeshires, Kyles, Lothians, Carricks and the men of Nidderdale and Annandale. Almost touching the head of Moor Lane and thronging in hundreds around the site of the monument were 3,000 Yorkshiremen and Scots under Lords Leven and Fairfax, supported on the Long Marston side of the monument by Sir Thomas Fairfax and Colonel Lambert commanding 4,500 horse. These, in turn, were facing across many acres of gorse the Royalist left wing of 5,000 cavalry under Goring and Lucas. These two great armies lay facing one another until about seven o'clock in the evening by which time Prince Rupert had given up the idea of a battle and was having an evening meal. He suddenly became aware of a long line of horsemen, led by Cromwell, descending Bilton Bream which joins up Marston Hill to Tockwith village.

Ashe wrote: "You might have seen the bravest sight, for they moved downhill in thick, coloured clouds in brigades 1,000 and 1,500 each." They came first at a glittering walk, then a trot and a hand gallop across the Tockwith road, and finally full gallop through hedge and ditch straight into Rupert's van. Surprised by this sudden and unexpected charge, it was minutes before the Royalists managed to re-form. All along the line the Parliamentary front was in action. Simultaneously with Cromwell's charge, Leslie's Scottish ponies —making little of the scrub—were into Rupert's flank. Lord Manchester's Foot, advancing in a running march, had crossed the ditch, as also had Lord Crawford. Within a few minutes the opposing Royalists, Grandison and Byron, were in the heart of the battle, Grandison's cavalry charging Cromwell with amazing gallantry. Further along towards the present day monument, Lord Leven's men were also in action, the Fairfaxes driving their raw recruits into Moor Lane where,

The charge of Cromwell's famous "Ironsides" at the Battle of Marston Moor, 1644.

met by a Royalist crossfire from behind the still-existing hedge, they charged the Whitecoats lower down. At the same time Cromwell—now wounded in the throat—seemed to be following the figures of a clock face, moving relentlessly from nine to ten, to eleven, and then to twelve. Having, driven Rupert's cavalry by sheer force along Wilstrop Wood—Cromwell seems to have awaited developments from the Parliamentary Right Wing under Fairfax.

Strange though it may seem, not a galloper or aide-de-camp appears to have been present on Marston Moor that evening, nor even a watcher on the hill. Under these circumstances, seeking to complete his own figure, Sir Thomas at the head of his 4,000 cavalry charged several times through the fatal scrub. Time and again his horses refused to go on. Three separate charges Fairfax made only to be thrown back by Goring. Finally at the head of only 400 picked horsemen, he

Scenes on Marston Moor. Above: The tall and grey monument to the battle. Opposite page, top: A view of the battlefield from Cromwell's Clump. Opposite page, bottom: Moor Lane, scene of most of the fighting.

broke through the ranks of Royalist horse, little doubt hoping that others would follow. This they failed to do and Fairfax, in charging at least a portion of Goring's cavalry and forcing them almost to the gates of York, returned to find himself alone and barred by a great bulk of Royalist horsemen. Goring, Urry and Lucas, together with what cavalry they could muster, wheeled to their own right, and fell apparently indiscriminately on the troops in Moor Lane. Fighting men of each side strove wildly to evacuate the lane, and Royalist and Puritan, Scottish and English, came "pouring like smoke" out on to the track beside the present day monument. In vain did the commanders seek to stem the flight, while across the track and over Marston Hill streamed men by the thousand consumed by panic fear. Last but by no means least fled the three Parliamentary generals—Lord Fairfax to Cawood Castle in order to make fresh plans, Manchester to leave the field but soon to return; Leven never to stop riding until he came to Leeds.

With the entire face of the battle counterchanged, and with thousands of Royalists thronging Marston Lane or ransacking the Parliamentary baggage wagons on the hill, news was sent off to the king at Oxford telling him of a tremendous Royalist victory. At the same time Sir Thomas Fairfax, out on the field with his face slashed by a sword cut, was slowly making his way towards Wilstrop Wood. Here, falling in with Cromwell and Sir David Leslie, he told of the terrible chaos and shambles of Marston Lane. "A good Commander of Horse," once wrote one of Cromwell's contemporaries, "is as rare as a good Commander in Chief and Cromwell was both." So it was on this occasion.

It was almost night with a rising moon when Cromwell and Leslie, attended by Fairfax and Lambert, rode swiftly across the face of Marston Moor at the head of the famous Ironsides and Manchester's Horse. They charged into a galloping mass of men, not only to annihilate the Royalist horse and foot in Marston Lane but, assisted by Manchester's Foot, to decimate the troops on the hill. "The Royalist bays were turned to willows, a day of trouble, rebuke and blasphemy at hand," noted Ashe. Late that night beneath a yellow moon scarcely a Royalist was left on the field, save only those needed to muster a terrible list of dead. In Whitesyke Close a thousand blood-soaked Whitecoats, refusing quarter, lay rank on rank to be buried a foot or so below the ground. Beside Wilstrop Wood were the Royalist slain—at least 3,000 out of 4,500 dead. Stripped of clothing that none should recognise their rank,

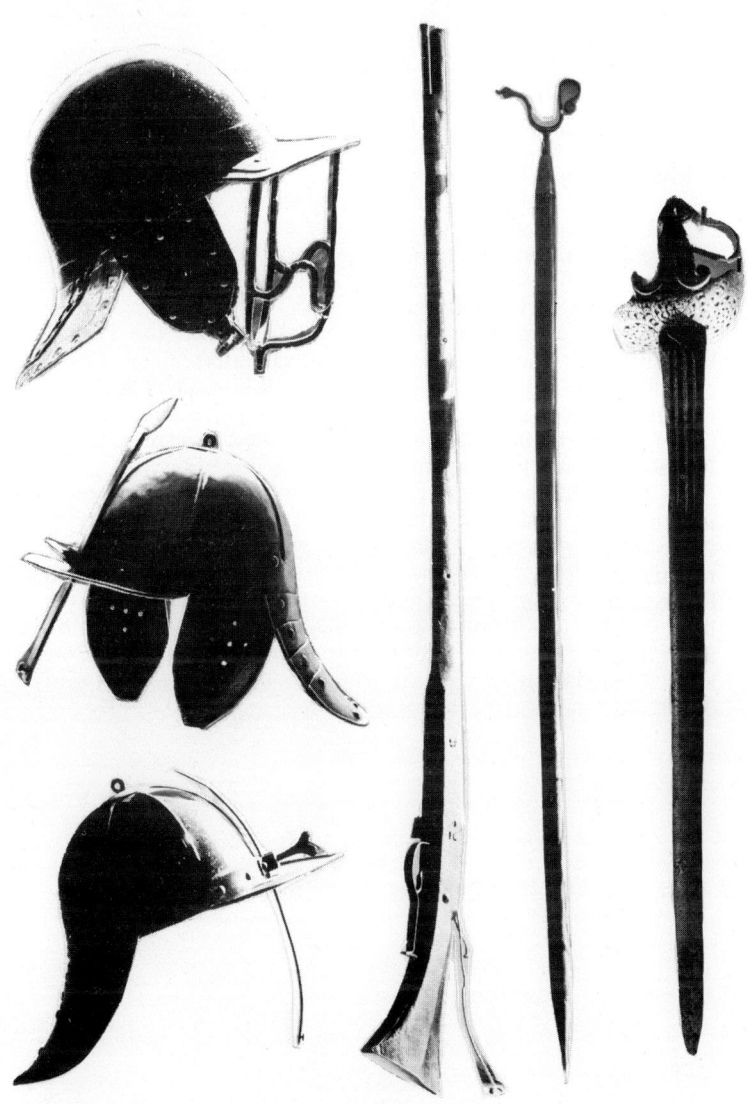

Relics of Marston Moor. Left: Helmets. Centre: Matchlock. Right: Broadsword. (Photos by courtesy of the Castle Museum, York).

dawn beheld Sir Charles Lucas, joint commander of the Royalist Left Wing and now a prisoner, slowly riding past the dead. "Alas," said he, refusing to recognise a single face, "Alas for King Charles, poor King Charles!"

Prince Rupert had escaped only by hiding in a beanfield, and once at York demanded sardonically, "And of Lord Newcastle, what will Lord Newcastle do?"

"I shall sail for Holland," answered the Marquis, "for I will not stay to abide the laughter of the Court."

"And what of Lord Eythin?"

"I," said Eythin, who like Newcastle loathed the Prince, "shall go with him. And what of your Highness?"

Coldly, ironically, yet with something of humour, the Prince is reputed to have replied, "My Lords, the Devil hath been in this. For me, I shall ride north and so into Lancashire, where I shall hope to fight again."

So ended Marston Moor. More than a century later workmen engaged in draining the Moor were to uncover many of those silent mounds. Today, conning the lists of slain, or reading of rings, bullets, sword-hilts or cannon shot which from time to time have been unearthed, one thinks of the dead of Marston Moor and pays silent tribute to men who on a summer's evening in a still-existing grassy lane altered the story of a nation.

Sources

General sources:
The Old History of Bradford (1776).
Roll Call of Boroughbridge (1830).
Pictorial History of the People, George Craik & Charles Macfarlane (Charles Knight, 1847).
Domesday Book for Yorkshire, Ellis (In Yorkshire Archaelogial Journal, 1877-9).
Jackson's Cyclist Guide to Yorkshire (1891).
Idle, J. H. Turner (1894).
Kirkby Overblow and District, R. Speight (1903).
The Old Kingdom of Elmet, Edmund Bogg (1906).
History of the English People, Greenwood. (Macmillan, 1921).
History and Topography of Bradford, John James.
Leeds Parish Registers.

General works on battles:
Battlefields of Yorkshire, W. Grainge (York, 1854).
Battles Fought in Yorkshire, A. D. H. Leadman (Bradbury, Agnew & Co., 1891).
Yorkshire Battles, E. Lamplough (Hull, 1891).
The Battlefields of England, A. H. Burn (1950).

Chs. 2 & 3:
See above.

Ch. 4:
See above.
The Great North Road, G. Harper (1902).

Ch. 5:

State Papers: Domestic (1566-79).

Nicholas Tempest (In Yorkshire Archaeological Journal, Vol. 11, 1891).

Rising of the North, W. E. Collins (Church Historical Society, 1891).

Memorials of the Rebellion, Sir C. Sharpe.

Rebellion of the Earls, R. R. Reid (In Royal Historical Society Transactions, Vol. 20).

Rising of the North, H. V. McCall (In Yorkshire Archaeological Journal, Vol. 18).

Ch. 6:

Memoirs of General Fairfax . . ., from the MS of Joseph Lister and others (Knaresborough, 1810).

History of the Civil Wars, S. R. Gardiner (London, 1886).

York Minster and Bootham Bar. Many thanksgiving services were held at at the Minster after battle victories.